The Government Manager's Guide to Project Management

The Government Manager's Essential Library

The Government Manager's Essential Library is a series of easy-to-use, subject-specific guides on issues every government manager faces:

The Government Manager's Guide to Project Management

JONATHAN WEINSTEIN, PMP
TIMOTHY JAQUES, PMP

MANAGEMENTCONCEPTSPRESS

MANAGEMENTCONCEPTS PRESS

8230 Leesburg Pike, Suite 800
Tysons Corner, Virginia 22182
Phone: 703.790.9595
Fax: 703.790.1371
www.managementconcepts.com

Printed in the United States of America

Library of Congress Control Number: 2013943145

ISBN 978-1-56726-417-3

ABOUT THE AUTHORS

Jonathan Weinstein, PMP, has worked in a variety of roles in both the project management and management consulting arenas. His project experience spans the private sector, from insurance to IT organizations, and the public sector, including agencies at all levels of government—local, state, and federal; civilian, and defense. Jon has been a featured speaker at U.S. and international conferences.

Timothy Jaques, PMP, focuses on helping clients tackle tough problems by applying the discipline of project management. He has worked in a variety of federal and state government agencies, where he has managed projects, developed project management methodologies and PMOs, and delivered training. Tim is a practitioner and advocate of organizational change management, especially in the project environment. He has also spoken and written on various aspects of project management and organizational change.

Jon and Tim are founding partners at Line of Sight (www.line-of-sight.com), which delivers project management, process reengineering, and organizational change management services to government and private-sector clients. They are coauthors of *Achieving Project Management Success in the Federal Government* and chapters in two books on project management.

CONTENTS

PREFACE

Projects pervade our everyday work and life, and governments have dealt in the realm of projects for as long as there have been governing bodies. The U.S. federal government has employed project management since its earliest days and in recent years has formalized the methods it uses to carry out a wide-ranging spectrum of projects.

This book is designed to be a useful tool for government managers. Our goal is not to provide an exhaustive enumeration of project management practices, but rather to offer a realistic cross section of the project management discipline—a "state of the practice" in the largest single enterprise in the world, the U.S. federal government. We hope this book will enlighten and serve to improve project management for federal leaders, project teams, and others who influence the direction of projects.

Describing project management within the federal government—its three branches, 15 departments, and myriad establishments, authorities, commissions, and corporations—is a study in frustration. On one level, project management is a function that has a clear set of objectives. Yet below the surface lies a complex and highly diverse web of organizational cultures, locations, missions, and funding streams. The forces that bind federal agencies together include a common set of laws and a dedication to continuous improvement.

The Government Manager's Guide to Project Management presents effective practices from organizations across a vast enterprise. Clearly, the tools and techniques employed by one organization are not necessarily a prescription for success in another. Key factors such as organizational culture, executive support, resource availability, staff capability, and the nature of the organization's services all contribute to the environment in which project management will either thrive or stagnate.

This book addresses the entire scope of project management, from organization to methodology, technology to leadership. We begin with a brief discussion of the evolution of—and the key organizations involved in—project management in the federal government (Chapter 1). We then address the three project management organizational dimensions of culture, systems, and structure (Chapter 2), the development and management of project teams (Chapter 3), and leveraging technology for project success in the federal environment (Chapter 4).

The next few chapters highlight practices and successes in the areas of communication (Chapter 5), project leadership (Chapter 6), stakeholders (Chapter 7), key competencies and skills (Chapter 8), and the federal project management framework, which encompasses governance, portfolio management, and methodology (Chapter 9).

We then address project performance management (Chapter 10). We conclude by considering the prospects for and promise of project management across the federal government (Chapter 11).

Our many conversations with project management leaders and practitioners throughout the federal government have convinced us that significant and important progress is being made that can be applied by the government manager in project management.

—Jon Weinstein

—Tim Jaques

ACKNOWLEDGMENTS

A modern-day sales expert cum philosopher, Jeffrey Gitomer, once said that the two most important things another person could give are time and attention. Researching and writing a book that covers the breadth of the U.S. government requires the contribution of time and attention by many individuals. We gratefully acknowledge the wellspring of information, candid discussion, and access to documents provided by so many dedicated federal employees and private sector personnel. We thank you for allowing us into your particular world of project management.

We wish to acknowledge Myra Strauss, editor extraordinaire. Thank you for many hours of thoughtful reading and edits, an open door policy, and tough criticism. We also wish to thank the Management Concepts staff and authors who supported our efforts.

We are greatly indebted to the Project Management Institute for providing us with excellent source material.

Finally, we simply could not have completed this book without our exceptional team of staff. We offer a special thanks to Julie Rodgers for holding down the fort and to Clare Skelly for her dogged determination in managing us through this effort. We also thank the entire Line of Sight team for providing us with many examples of inspired project management in the work they do each day with our clients. This was a team effort, and we thank the entire team for pushing us forward and covering our backs.

Chapter 1

THE EVOLUTION OF FEDERAL PROJECT MANAGEMENT

We need to internalize this idea of excellence.

— PRESIDENT BARACK OBAMA

Throughout history mankind has labored to achieve amazing feats that defy our imagination: the great pyramids of Giza, the Taj Mahal, the Great Wall of China, the D-Day invasion. Human beings—and governments—naturally seek to apply resources toward the creation of monuments, public works, and war. Although such efforts have spanned thousands of years, only in the past 60 years has the discipline of project management come to be formally recognized and defined.

The U.S. Government Accountability Office (GAO) describes the federal government as "the world's largest and most complex entity."[1] In terms of scale, the federal government expended over $3.5 trillion in fiscal year 2012 on operations and myriad projects to develop and provide new products and services—from bridge construction to aircraft development, from AIDS awareness to nuclear material disposal. The expenditure of these funds represents the single largest government marketplace in the world, employing many millions of people directly or indirectly.

The U.S. government is a massive machine, yet no single central civilian entity has the authority for establishing, promoting, or enforcing standards and guidelines for the project management discipline across the federal government enterprise. The absence of this authority is not the result of a conscious decision to allow different agencies and departments to adopt the system that works best for their particular circumstances. Rather, project management within the federal government has grown and thrived seemingly at random, developing idiosyncratically in the various agencies, laboratories, and field offices where the federal government works and where support for project management is strong.

PROJECTS IN THE FEDERAL SECTOR

What is a project? The classic definition is a temporary endeavor undertaken to create a unique product, service, or result. The product, service, or result is developed through a specific effort that includes a beginning, middle, and end. A project is different from a program, which has two general definitions in the federal government. We define *program* as a group of related projects that are managed in a harmonized way and contribute to the achievement of a common goal. A program often includes elements of ongoing work or work related to specific deliverables. A vivid historical example is the Apollo program, which encompassed distinct projects aimed at developing a vehicle, buildings, control hardware and software, etc. The government also uses *program* to mean a continuing overall operation or grouping of services, such as Medicaid or the Small Business Administration's loan guaranty program.

Projects satisfy a deeply held need in the human psyche to commune and conquer. Projects are designed to create change and are at once logistical, political, physical, and mental. They demand our attention and require us to work toward a common goal. Projects are the manifestation of hope—a wish for things to be better in the future if we work hard enough—combined with the need to carry out a finite activity, to set measurable goals and objectives, and to be able to declare success when the goals are reached and the objectives are met.

When everyday work is performed, we invoke the mechanisms of process management. When current work is aimed at achieving a specific goal or objective, the mechanisms of project management—scoping, scheduling, and measuring—are involved in an effort to increase the likelihood of success and realize our ambitions for some future achievement.

Manager Alert

Infusing project management within an organization that views work as process management is as much a cultural transformation as it is a procedural one.

Project management asks us to measure twice and cut once. Philosophically this approach makes sense, but when measuring twice costs millions of dollars and takes many years, the demands on a project intensify. The forces that drive project management are largely contextual, evoked by the mission and structure of the host organization. The dynamics in the federal sector revolve around authority and power, scarcity and abundance (two elements that frequently cohabit in an organization), and change readiness and acceptance. Other factors come into play as well, and for these reasons, no two organizations will follow the same exact style of project management.

Projects in the federal sector differ in many ways from projects in other sectors or industries. The Project Management Institute (PMI)[2] has identified several factors that affect how project management works in the public sector,[3] particularly for large projects:

1. *A wide array of important stakeholders is involved.* Projects may involve input from or output to world leaders, Congress, high-ranking appointees, taxpayers, policymakers, special interest groups, and others. Managing powerful constituencies increases project complexity and invokes new dimensions of communication management.

2. *Project outcomes often have great consequences.* Launching spaceships, consolidating military bases, developing a vaccine to fight a pandemic, and building billion-dollar bridges all represent potentially significant public consequences. Because public projects are highly visible, a failure can live on for a generation or more.

3. *The revolving political landscape means constant change.* New administrations arrive every four years. Congress is in a state of gridlock while shifting priorities with the changing political winds, and agency leadership changes frequently. With each political cycle comes a new or revised set of priorities, legislation, and often a new approach to management. Civil servants and appointees are challenged to work together to effect change in the context of current political and ongoing organizational priorities.

4. *Public scrutiny magnifies mistakes.* Publicly funded projects must endure— indeed, must embrace—a continuous open window to the public. The public includes individual citizens, special interest groups, nongovernmental organizations (NGOs), and corporate interests. While some federal projects are shielded from continuous external inspection, freedom of information laws and the public sentiment can influence a project manager's approach or the project's execution or outcomes.

5. *Dramatic failures can lead to intense oversight.* Examples of "extreme" failures in federal projects (such as the response to Hurricane Katrina and oversight of the financial industry) often elicit intense reactions from key stakeholders, especially Congress. However, project management is a highly contextual field and Congress has not yet adopted laws specific to project management practices.

Past legislative attempts have sought to establish trigger points for greater oversight, even project cancellation, if major projects begin to fail, as with Senate Bill 3384, the

Information Technology Investment Oversight Enhancement and Waste Prevention Act of 2008. Even in the absence of legislation, however, it is possible to codify the structural components of project management, and the federal government has been moving steadily toward instituting more formalized processes.

In this context, project management in the federal government is both exciting and challenging. Successful project managers must deal with the realities of fickle priorities, political administrations, tenuous budgets, and the tangled web of regulations, laws, and policies that direct federal activities. Yet the federal government, with all its subordinate agencies, departments, administrations, and commissions, still must take the long road to successful project management, implementing one piece at a time. How did such a complicated environment come into being?

THE EVOLUTION OF PROJECT MANAGEMENT IN THE FEDERAL GOVERNMENT

The government has used documented planning techniques since the earliest days of the nation. Journals, lists, and diagrams characterized planning documents dating back to the late 1700s. These documents often took the form of correspondence regarding administrative details.

The term *project* did not come into its current usage until the early 20th century. Throughout the nation's early years, *project* meant something akin to an undertaking, an endeavor, or a purpose. Compare that with today's dictionary definition of the word, "a collaborative enterprise, frequently involving research or design, that is carefully planned to achieve a particular aim,"[4] or PMI's more focused definition, "a temporary endeavor undertaken to create a unique product, service or result."[5]

Over the next 120 years, the management of projects evolved in engineering, construction, scientific endeavors, and other increasingly knowledge-centric fields. Although there was little apparent emphasis on project management as a discipline, many of the foundational concepts of management were forming at this time. Formalized project management evolved out of the management theory emerging during the industrial revolution, when concepts like standardization, quality control, work planning, and assembly construction were beginning to take hold.

In 1911, Frederick Taylor published the seminal work *Principles of Scientific Management*, in which he defined many of the elements of project management today: task planning and instruction, job specialization, and effective supervision. Taylor's worldview emanated from the factory, and his theories shifted the emphasis from the worker's role of defining and resolving task problems to the manager's role of significantly influencing task problems. The federal government adopted these private sector-based theories and management paradigms, creating multilayered organizations staffed by managers of managers. Where manufacturing organizations were organized around assembly lines, government organizations were organized into self-contained and organized units, some oriented functionally and some operationally.

A colleague of Taylor's, Henry Gantt, worked alongside Taylor literally and figuratively in the development of modern management theory. Gantt's ideas greatly influenced key project management theories in use today. In particular, his ideas on work planning have contributed to modern scheduling practices. Working with production facilities that were developing weaponry and goods for the U.S. government, Gantt understood that production and assembly work was sequenced, segmented, and measurable. He devised a concept called the "balance of work," which presented work as measurable units. Workers were required to fulfill a day's quota of work. This work could be reduced to a plan and laid out on a graphical horizon, which later became known as the Gantt chart.

Project management began to take on its modern form after World War II. The first substantial evidence of government-based project management was the Navy's *Polaris* missile project, initiated in 1956 as part of the fleet ballistic missile program, with Lockheed Missile Systems Division as the prime contractor. The *Polaris* project delivered a truly complex product, the most advanced submarine-based nuclear missile of the day, at a time when the United States was determined to win the nuclear arms race.

The use of multiple major contracts for one product was a new development. There were no tools for integrating the various contracts and understanding the impact on the overall program of schedule changes by contractors. To address the complexity and uncertainty associated with *Polaris*, the Navy's special projects office developed the project evaluation and review technique (PERT). PERT was a key element in an "integrated planning and control system for the Fleet Ballistic Missile program."[6]

Other optimization practices were developed during the 1950s, including the line of balance (LOB) programming model, which preceded PERT, and the management operation system technique (MOST), which improved on PERT estimates. The commonly used work breakdown structure (WBS), a multilevel outline of the work to be performed within a project, was introduced as a concept in concert with the implementation of PERT and came into formal use in the early 1960s.[7] With the development of these new planning and reporting tools to assist in the management and integration of major weapons system components, the project management discipline demonstrated that truly complex endeavors could be estimated and organized effectively. It was during this period that the term *project management* was coined.

In a concentrated effort to address the increasing complexity of projects, several other key concepts emerged during these early years. The DuPont Corporation developed critical path methodology (CPM) in 1957 to support the construction and maintenance of chemical plants. DuPont and the Remington Rand corporations jointly developed an algorithmic approach to schedule development using the UNIVAC computer developed by Rand. The idea was to feed activity schedules into a computer, let the computer create the project schedule, and thereby reveal the critical versus noncritical tasks. The network of activities defined which tasks would materially delay the project and which would not. As schedule revisions occurred, CPM could be used to calculate the new set of critical tasks.

In the early 1960s, the Air Force, Army, Navy, and Defense Supply Agency jointly developed the cost and schedule control system criteria (C/SCSC) approach as a way to gain better access into large, contractor-run projects. The *Minuteman* project was plagued with cost and schedule overruns—and a contractor that was reluctant to share project performance data with its customer. In 1967, the Department of Defense (DoD) established a set of 35 criteria, grouped into five major categories that allowed government contract managers to understand schedule performance and cost performance. C/SCSC resulted in the core elements of what was to be eventually renamed earned value management (EVM).

The end of the 20th century was an interesting time to be involved in project management. Engineers with interest in management were given responsibility for running projects. Project management was in its early stages as a stand-alone discipline. Throughout the 1960s and 1970s, project management became the focus of increased intellectual endeavors. The number of academic papers, journals, and new ideas exploded, many of which focused on federal government projects. In 1969 PMI was founded on the premise that the practices inherent in managing projects spanned a wide range of disciplines, from aeronautics to bridges to computer design and beyond.

Whereas the federal government led early development in modern project management, private industry and academia led after the 1970s. The construction industry boomed in the 1980s, leading to major advances in estimating and logistics. The emergence of the personal computer enabled individual project managers to automate planning and control activities themselves, rather than rely solely on project personnel. Of course, on the larger projects, planning and control staffs were still essential.

Throughout the 1970s and 1980s, the government adopted many of these new practices. In 1976, the Office of Management and Budget (OMB) issued Circular A-109, the first federal directive to address program management. This document solidified the role of C/SCSC in federal projects. Circular A-109 and the C/SCSC practices remained in place until 1996, when A-109 underwent a major revision. The development and revision of federal guidance related to project management was a clear sign that practices implemented within various civilian and defense organizations were being codified for government-wide use.

The 1990s saw a big push for governmental accountability and reform. Political winds drove key legislation that introduced strategic planning, the chief information officer role, and technology planning. Large technology projects were prone to delay and failure, requiring increased visibility, management, and justification. In response, OMB introduced a series of requirements dealing with capital and technology expenditures, reporting, and management. In June 2002, OMB issued regulations that applied to major acquisitions and major IT systems or projects that required the implementation of earned value management systems using the American National Standard Institute standards (ANSI/EIA 748-A-1998),[8] officially ending reliance on C/SCSC.

PROJECT MANAGEMENT IN GOVERNMENT TODAY

Now is an exciting time to be a project management practitioner in the federal government. Project management is reaching a new level of maturity and recognition as a critical skill set. The project management career is on the rise. A new breed of manager is emerging—one that was raised on the precepts of project management. Federal project management is evolving from a purely homespun set of practices into a formal discipline. Evidence of this evolution abounds:

- *Organizations are seeking to balance technical expertise with project management competencies*, often having to decide whether to assign technical experts to manage projects or skilled project managers to lead highly technical projects. Achieving this balance raises the question of what is more important in managing a project—expertise in the discipline or in the subject matter of the project.

- *In the past several years, the federal government has begun to promote agencies' development of an internal certification process for project and program managers.* This trend, coupled with the emergence of "new" skills that integrate with "traditional" skills (e.g., negotiation, facilitation, personnel management), is placing demands on federal project managers to adjust and adapt to new project environments. Acquiring and honing these skills will be essential for project managers and projects to achieve success.

- *Legislative and policy efforts have introduced greater oversight into large projects.* This increased oversight has contributed to advancements in project performance measurement, including the development and implementation of EVM practices.

- *Project management technologies have advanced to form a system that supports the full lifecycle of projects,* from concept and planning to implementation, operations, and maintenance.

Manager Alert

Federal project management is evolving from an ad hoc set of activities into a more formal discipline.

Despite these achievements in project management, challenges will continue to limit the ability of the federal government to manage projects successfully. These challenges include the following:

- *Project size.* Despite difficult economic times, there is no shortage of large-scale projects. Both civilian and defense agencies are in the throes of planning and implementing projects that are large in scale, scope, budget, and importance. Many of these projects represent the collaborative efforts of multiple organizations, yet personnel are not familiar with the concepts of project management.

- *Intervention into troubled projects.* With no consistent approach for escalating, intervening in, and resolving projects in crisis, agencies often must take steps to fix troubled projects without clear guidance. Timely intervention, as early in the project lifecycle as possible, is a critical success factor for troubled projects, yet often agency leaders do not have sufficient insight into the project or the knowledge and experience to understand the warning signals at an early stage.

- *Managing through the bureaucracy.* Project success often depends on the ability to remain nimble and free of classic bureaucratic constraints. The federal government has yet to define protocols and safeguards that will allow projects to move quickly when needed, eliminating unnecessary or burdensome activities while still adhering to checks and balances to protect project investments.

- *Mission diversity.* The diversity of missions presents a challenge for establishing enterprise project management structures and practices in many large agencies. To operate effectively in the face of this diversity, project management expertise must permeate the organization and be adapted to the "local" environment.

- *Acquisition vs. project management.* OMB has developed policies that promote sound and consistent acquisition policies across the federal government. The introduction and implementation of the federal acquisition certification for program and project managers (FAC-P/PM) is an example of efforts to foster greater linkages between the acquisition and project management specialties.

- *Unpredictable funding.* Many government projects can't count on their budgets being fully funded from year to year. If recent experience is a guide, this will be the norm rather than the exception. Some simply hope for the best and plan that the money will be there, while others spend precious time planning and developing "what-if" scenarios to address possible variations in funding levels.

- *Resource allocation, capacity, and capability.* Increasing project complexity demands increased project management capabilities. The "inventory" of trained or certified project managers does not meet the demand in most federal organizations, so on-the-job training is common. Assigning the right project manager to the right project at the right time remains a challenge for many government organizations.

The federal project management environment is rife with successes, challenges, and opportunities.

WHO'S WHO IN FEDERAL PROJECT MANAGEMENT

Numerous organizations are involved in the development of project management-related policies or the promotion of best practices. Some are formal government organizations, and others are groups or associations organized around a topic or a particular role.

Office of Management and Budget

Part of the executive branch, OMB supports the President in developing and implementing the federal budget. OMB also oversees executive branch agencies and ensures the effectiveness of agency programs. As part of this mission, OMB has played an integral role in developing project management guidance at the organizational and individual levels. Working primarily through acquisition rules and regulations, OMB has made significant contributions toward the development of a federal standard for project management.

Within OMB, the Office of Federal Procurement Policy (OFPP) is the primary driver of government-wide project management practices. OFPP was created in 1974 to administer federal procurement policies. Today, the office plays a key role in defining how large projects are reviewed and rated.

Manager Alert

The Office of Federal Procurement Policy is a driver of government-wide project management practices.

Government Accountability Office

As a result of large wartime expenditures and a public outcry for greater accountability, GAO, originally known as the General Accounting Office, was created under the Budget and Accounting Act of 1921.[9] GAO has long served a critical audit function in the U.S. government. GAO strives to help federal agencies improve performance, ensure accountability, and meet statutory requirements.

GAO has a major impact on projects across the federal government through its audit and review function. GAO evaluates hundreds of projects annually—projects of all sizes and in all areas of expertise. It maintains a "high-risk" list of large-scale projects that are failing to meet the objectives set by the planning team. GAO maintains reports on thousands of failed or endangered projects.

Chief Information Officers Council

The CIO Council (www.cio.gov) provides a venue for interagency best practice and information sharing on information technology. Originally established in 1996 by Executive Order 13011, the CIO Council was codified into law by Congress in the E-Government Act of 2002. The CIO Council comprises a number of committees that address all aspects of federal IT, including project management.

The council issues memos and work products that address improving IT project management. It also maintains a list of training resources, survey results, and other information that can assist agencies in advancing project management.

Federal Acquisition Institute

Established in 1976, the Federal Acquisition Institute (FAI) (www.fai.gov) "facilitates career development and strategic human capital management in support of a professional federal acquisition workforce."[10] FAI has developed a certification program for federal project and program managers. Dubbed the "federal acquisition certification for program and project managers," or FAC-P/PM, this certification establishes a set of baseline competencies and related requirements. The FAC-P/PM certification is relatively new, but it is being adopted by a host of agencies.

Project Management Institute

PMI (www.pmi.org) is a nongovernment, global association of project management practitioners with a membership of more than 265,000 across 170 countries. PMI offers a set of credentials corresponding to different specialties, such as project management, program management, and scheduling. PMI supports a number of programs aimed at the federal government. First and foremost is the Washington, D.C., PMI chapter. As the largest PMI chapter in the world, it offers an active membership a wide array of programs and symposiums.

The PMI government community of practice is a virtual community that brings together elected and civil servant government officials, as well as contractors and others, for the purpose of improving the management of projects in the public sector. The PMI® Roundtable is a government-focused venue for information and practice sharing. The PMI® Forum is an executive-level environment for discussing strategic and leadership issues in project management. PMI also advocates for the profession through its Washington, D.C., office.

CHALLENGES AHEAD FOR PROJECT MANAGEMENT IN THE FEDERAL GOVERNMENT

At the heart of project management today are questions that have yet to be answered to the satisfaction of skeptics. As indicated by in-depth studies by PMI and others, efforts are still being undertaken to determine whether project management delivers value. In the case of the federal government, is value returned to the taxpayer in the form of improved services, more modern infrastructures, or a stronger economy? Answering this fundamental question will enable the dialogue to shift toward considering the answers that will improve the project management discipline—which tools to use, when to use them, and the best way to use them in the federal government environment.

Describing project management within the numerous and diverse agencies, departments, authorities, and commissions of the federal government is daunting. On one level, project management is a function that has a clear set of objectives. Yet below the surface is a complex and highly diverse web of organizational cultures, missions, funding streams, and geography. The forces that bind federal agencies together include a common set of procurement laws and regulations, while other forces—the myriad legislative and appropriations requirements—demand that they work separately.

The practical experiences of federal project managers, sponsors, and executives speak to these issues and trends. President Obama's suggestion that we need to internalize the idea of excellence not only offers a challenge to the federal workforce but also describes the efforts underway in many government agencies today: making excellence the standard for managing projects.

NOTES

1.   www.gao.gov/products/GAO-09-271 (accessed April 2013).

2.   PMI, PMBOK, PMP, CAPM, and OPM3 are registered marks, and PgMP is a mark of the Project Management Institute, Inc.

3.   "Project Management in the Public Sector," www.pmi.org/Knowledge-Center/Publications-PM-Network/Feature-ProjectManagementinthePublicSector.aspx (accessed May 2013); see also

the *Government Extension to the PMBOK® Guide, Third Edition* (Newtown Square, PA: Project Management Institute, 2006).

4.   *Oxford English Dictionary,* online edition, "project," www.askoxford.com/concise_oed/project?view=uk.

5.   Project Management Institute, *A Guide to the Project Management Body of Knowledge (PMBOK® Guide), Fifth Edition* (Newtown Square, PA: Project Management Institute, 2013).

6.   Gregory T. Haugan, *Project Planning and Scheduling* (Vienna, VA: Management Concepts, 2002), p. 28.

7.   Gregory T. Haugan, *The Work Breakdown Structure in Government Contracting* (Vienna, VA: Management Concepts, 2003), pp. 7–9.

8.   American National Standards Institute, "Earned Value Management System." ANSI/EIA-748-B, June 2007.

9.   www.gao.gov/about/history/index.html (accessed April 2013).

10. www.fai.gov (accessed April 2013).

Chapter 2

FITTING PROJECT MANAGEMENT INTO THE ORGANIZATION

> *There are no problems we cannot solve together, and very few that we can solve by ourselves.*
>
> —PRESIDENT LYNDON BAINES JOHNSON

Successful project management in federal agencies must address project management across three organizational dimensions: culture, systems, and structure:

- *Culture* refers to the behaviors, attitudes and beliefs, language, and organizational rituals in place within a work setting. Culture describes the human environment, which may enhance or inhibit the success of project management.

- *Systems* connotes a related set of activities, processes, technologies, and supporting materials organized around a specific objective or desired outcome.

- *Structure* refers to the configuration of business units, divisions, directorates, and other constructs that make up an organization.

These three dimensions collectively define the environment within which project management will either thrive or wane.

When one or more of these dimensions is ignored, unintended consequences can result (see Table 2-1). For example, if the organizational structure is not in alignment with the supporting systems, informal processes and "back channels" may be relied on to get work done. When the organizational structure is misaligned with the culture, the environment may favor loud personalities rather than sound thinking. Likewise, a lack of systems may lead to unclear roles and responsibilities across units: The culture may reward heroic individual or team contributions rather than the steady individual or team that is consistently on time and on budget. Finally, if the culture is not properly aligned toward a project management environment, project management may not be recognized as a legitimate function and significant organizational resistance may arise.

TABLE 2-1 Consequences of Ignoring Key Dimensions of Project Management			
A Lack of . . .	Can Lead to . . .		
	Structure	Systems	Culture
Supporting culture	Project management not recognized as legitimate	Organizational resistance, lack of effective sponsorship	
Alignment with systems	Unclear roles and responsibilities		Heroic efforts rewarded
Aligned structure		Shadow systems used; back channels required	Dominant personalities valued

CULTURE

Project management is a discipline that naturally reflects the culture of the organization. Projects leverage the people, processes, and systems within the organization, all of which are imbued with facets of the culture. *Culture* can be defined as the confluence of behaviors, attitudes and beliefs, language, and rituals that form the basis for a "normal" experience in an organization.

How can understanding culture help a project management practice? An effective project management practice must align itself culturally within its environment. This does not mean that it can never impose change or go against the grain; projects are often at the forefront of change. To be successful in the federal environment, a project management orientation must be absorbed into the culture and adopted. It must operate within the normative ranges behaviorally, in its underlying attitude, in its language, and in its adherence to ritual.

Manager Alert

If the culture is not properly aligned toward a project management environment, significant organizational resistance is likely.

SYSTEMS

Systems is a broad-based term that connotes a related set of activities, processes, technologies, and supporting materials organized around a specific objective or desired outcome. Examples of systems in an organization include resource management, service delivery, contract management, and communication.

Organizational systems can be documented, formal processes or age-old methods for getting things done. Regardless, projects must be able to access and use the various technical and process-based systems that enable an organization to function. To be successful, project management must access these systems and be able to interact with them in ways that support the organization.

As a relatively new arrival in many agency hierarchies, project management faces the challenge of integrating with long-held anchor systems such as human resources, finance, contracts, and operations. Project managers must be able to leverage human resource processes in hiring staff, assigning project resources, or providing support for necessary training. In the federal sector, there is no best practice for how a project management practice should integrate within these systems. Yet projects must operate across existing systems and silos to retain resources and achieve results (see Figure 2-1).

Organizational units are vertically focused on their functional mission. However, the typical project runs horizontally across the organization to access resources from a number of areas. For project management to succeed, it must have access to systems within the organizational units. These systems include processes, core operations, and technology—any type of common workflow that results in a standard organizational deliverable or result. Successful agencies in the federal sector have defined clear boundaries and processes for using existing systems. PMO directors have established relationships with their counterparts in human resources, finance, and contracts to ensure that requests are handled properly.

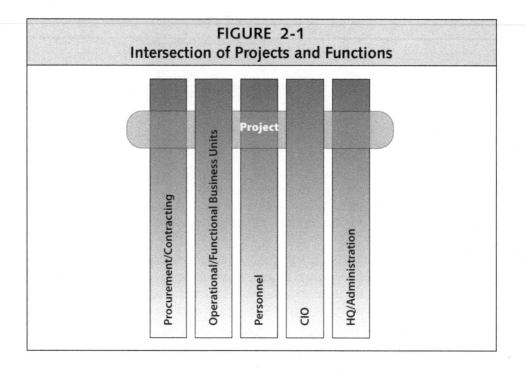

FIGURE 2-1
Intersection of Projects and Functions

Manager Alert

More and more, projects tend to run horizontally across the organization, accessing resources from multiple areas.

STRUCTURE

Structure represents the most formal connection between project management and the organization (think of an organization chart). The structure of an organization should reflect long-term goals as well as recognition of services, delivery models, and alignment of staff. While structure is often difficult to establish initially, it may be the easiest organizational dimension to change.

Unlike culture and systems, changing structure is a matter of moving reporting responsibilities, staffing, and physical space to accommodate a new set of priorities. This is no small feat and should not be minimized by suggesting it is simple. Yet, structure is one area where relatively fast changes can be made to accommodate a function like project management.

Project management must be anchored appropriately to the organization. Federal agencies display a wide range of organizational configurations of project management. All project managers are part of some type of reporting structure, although the details will vary from agency to agency and department to department. In some cases, projects report through a chief information officer (CIO). Other organizations have projects reporting up through the administrative function or chief administrative officer (CAO) or across a variety of executive lines. This variation is a natural result of the influences and forces that project management must address in becoming established and growing within an organization, including economics, intra-agency politics, external politics (i.e., dealing with elected officials), physical space, alignment with mission, and the sense of criticality of project management.

Where the project management practice developed naturally in an organization, it often evolves as shadow processes with no clear lines of authority. While a bottom-up approach serves early project management practices well, these practices must eventually become properly linked to the organization or risk being seen as an intrusion and disruption. Once established within the structure of the organization, project management can operate legitimately and projects can be properly sponsored and staffed. Ideally, a way will be found to combine the entrepreneurial spirit with the organizational strength of an established project management system.[1]

The project management office and the program management office are the mainstay business structures through which projects are channeled in the federal government. (Keep in mind that the term *program* in federal parlance often represents an ongoing operation that is legislatively mandated, such as Medicare. The traditional project management definition of *program* is a series of projects or related subprojects.)

Manager Alert

The project management office and the program management office can be important business structures through which projects are effectively executed in the federal government.

The PMO typically is a permanent organizational unit chartered to coordinate project resources and improve overall project success. Three general models are commonly found in the federal environment:

- *Center of excellence.* This type of organization is typically a support unit, providing information, best practices, mentoring, and coordination services. A center of excellence has no direct authority for projects and does not maintain direct responsibility for the organization's project managers. The focus of this model is to provide the framework and increase the opportunity for project success, with an emphasis on methodology and competency development.

- *Functional or delivery-oriented PMO.* Many PMOs are created within a division or directorate to satisfy that particular area's project needs. In an IT PMO, for example, the information technology organization maintains a PMO to plan and deploy its projects effectively. This PMO type may also be charged with ensuring adherence to organizational standards, policies, and procedures, with an emphasis on compliance and audits. This model focuses on ensuring that projects are "done right."

- *Strategic PMO.* With time and success, PMOs can contribute to the formation and execution of an organization's strategy. The strategic PMO implements the activities associated with most or all of the elements on each tier. Overall, the focus of this PMO is to initiate projects and programs that are aligned with the organization's mission and strategy. Strategic PMOs require close collaboration and strong engagement with executives and are oriented toward investment decision-making, determining where the organization's limited resources will be focused, and which projects and programs will contribute to mission realization. This PMO type is focused on getting the "right projects" done.

The program management office (PgMO) is often established to meet a specific program's objectives. For example, in replacing a legacy system over a period of five years, the PgMO is a useful organizational construct that provides a legitimate home for the various projects that fall under this initiative. Once the program objectives are met, the office is disbanded.

For all but a few mission-focused organizations like NASA and parts of DoD, program management practices have not yet been fully integrated. Owing in part to the disparate definitions of the term *program,* there is no standard configuration for a PgMO within the federal government. Each federal department or agency defines its own configuration of program management as a function within the organization.

NOTE

1. See Paul Roberts, *Guide to Project Management* (London: The Economist and Profile Books, 2007), pp. 42–69; and Rick A. Morris, *The Everything Project Management Book* (Avon, MA: Avon Media, 2002), pp. 101–108.

Chapter 3

BUILDING STRONG
TEAMS

Teamwork is the ability to work together toward a common vision. The ability to direct individual accomplishments toward organizational objectives. It is the fuel that allows common people to attain uncommon results.

—ANDREW CARNEGIE

M anagers cannot do all the work of their teams; if they could, there would be no need for teams. Even the 19th century industrialist Andrew Carnegie knew that, as much as he would have liked to do everything himself, he needed others. One of the project manager's or leader's key responsibilities in both the federal government and the private sector is to ensure that team members work well with each other and are able to perform their individual jobs.

TEAM TYPES AND STRUCTURES

The particular structure of the team will depend on the task, the organization or agency, and the people available (see Figure 3-1). The ideal staffing for a task or project simply may not be possible.

One immediate issue is team size. A small team will generally be easier to manage effectively because the project manager will be able to get to know team members better. In the initial phase of the project, the manager will be seeking team member "buy-in" to the project's goals and objectives. With fewer team members, the manager may be able to link team goals to individual goals more effectively.

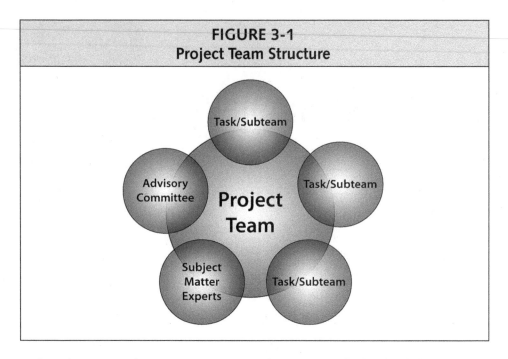

FIGURE 3-1
Project Team Structure

Technical project realities may necessitate a large team, which is by definition more complicated to manage: the more people, the more possible interrelationships. As the number of team members expands arithmetically, the number of possible interrelationships expands geometrically, creating more and more relationships and therefore potential complications.

The project manager has to take the "math" of interrelationships and communication into account when forming the team. First and foremost, managers have to consider whether they can handle a large team. Will the project manager be spending so much time managing interrelationships and communication that there will be little time left to manage the project? Forming project subteams around major tasks is an effective method for harnessing large teams, with the managers of those subteams reporting directly to the overall project manager. Selecting the right team type or structure is an important consideration for the project manager.

Manager Alert

One of the project manager's key responsibilities is to ensure that team members work well with each other and are able to perform their individual jobs.

Most projects use a matrix team construct, employing a cross-functional team comprising resources temporarily assigned from other parts of the organization. Many organizations find that this structure promotes cross-functional solutions and enhances professional growth opportunities. As with any construct, however, the matrix team has its challenges. Project staff who are "borrowed" for the project have to answer to multiple managers, work with new team members, and balance the work of the project with their "day job." For project managers, getting the right personnel resources when they're needed from other units in the organization can be a real challenge. On the flip side, the resource's functional (or line) managers often lament the loss of control over their direct reports' assignments and professional development.

While the matrix team is common for federal projects, two other team structures seen with growing frequency in the federal environment are the integrated project team and the virtual team. Each offers unique contributions to success in an increasingly complex project environment.

Integrated Project Team

Use of an integrated project team (IPT) is growing across civilian federal organizations, mirroring the growing complexity of projects in the federal government. Project managers using an IPT structure will need to advance their fundamental skills as they build new competencies to be successful in the evolving project management environment.

IPTs can be formed at two "levels": project-based, with representation from all teams responsible for the execution of a project or program; and functionally based, with representation from all key stakeholder groups. The Department of Energy (DOE), in Order 413.3A, adopted a project-based approach, defining IPTs as "cross-functional groups of individuals organized for the specific purpose of delivering a project to an external or internal customer."[1] DOE's related guidance on IPTs aptly identifies them as "the crossroads where the technical, management, budgetary, safety, and security meet."[2]

DOE decided that "all acquisition programs and projects shall use an integrated project team approach to managing projects." DOE promoted IPTs as the "core of project management implementation," coordinating all essential acquisition activities "through the use of multi-disciplined teams, from requirements definition through production, fielding/deployment, and operational support in order to optimize design, manufacturing, business, and supportability processes."[3] The idea of the IPT is to integrate and coordinate activities and to maximize overall project performance rather than performance in particular functional areas.

The IPT is intended to be flexible; thus, DOE's regulations did not call for specific team membership and organization. DOE did, however, remind project and IPT managers of three basic core elements: "(1) the PD [project director] is in charge of their own project; (2) IPTs are responsible to and empowered by the PD; and (3) communication between IPTs, the PD, the Program Manager and all levels of acquisition is encouraged to exchange information, build trust, and resolve issues—ideally at the lowest possible level."[4]

Virtual Team

A virtual team comprises members "linked via the Internet or media channels to each other and various project partners, such as contractors, customers, and regulators. Although physically separated, technology links these individuals so they can share information and operate as a unified project team."[5] Because large projects and the federal agencies that execute them tend to be geographically dispersed, virtual teams are being relied on increasingly. On the positive side, day-to-day annoyances and distractions may be minimized with a virtual team. But how, for example, can meetings be scheduled in different time zones? What is lost when face-to-face contact is not possible? In addressing issues like this, the project manager's dual goal is to design and structure the team well *and* to get the team to function well.

Project managers must be able to adapt to working in a virtual environment. Important skills and actions include the following:

- Coaching and managing performance without the traditional forms of feedback.

- Selecting and appropriately using the right communication and collaboration technologies.

- Leading in a cross-cultural environment by understanding the impact of various team members' cultural characteristics on the virtual team setting. The relationship between the project organization's culture and the deployment of virtual teams should also be considered.

- Facilitating team members' transition into the virtual work environment. Work standards will likely be more complex than those in a conventional office.

- Building and maintaining trust, to an even greater degree than on a conventional team. The initial project buy-in will have to include work methods as well as project goals.

- Networking across standard organizational and hierarchical boundaries. The result may be breaking through organizational boundaries and increasing cross-departmental collaboration.

- Developing and adapting organizational processes to meet the expanded demands of the team.[6] One method to consider is allowing virtual team members to determine their own reporting schedules and methods.[7] Before doing so, however, project managers must obtain (or validate that they have) the necessary authority to make process changes. Rejected process changes can result in a loss of credibility.

- Communicating the value of the virtual team to stakeholders while communicating the value of the project itself.

Manager Alert

The project manager's dual goal is to design and structure the team well *and* to facilitate the team's effective functioning.

ESTABLISHING THE PROJECT TEAM

Teamwork can be defined as a "cooperative effort by the members of a group or team to achieve a common goal."[8] In general, team members contribute to project success by bringing different and complementary skills to the effort to achieve project goals. One of the project manager's critical first tasks is to choose the personnel best suited for the task and to get them to "sign on" to the task, that is, to make the project's goals their goals.

The first step, after the project itself is created, is to select and establish the team. The project manager may not have the option to fully determine who will join the team and may have to work with staff already on hand. Ideally, the project manager should be able to select individuals who have the technical skills to contribute to the team and who can work well with each other. Highly skilled prima donnas may have skills that contribute to the general work of an agency, but they are best suited to work on projects that can be done independently.

Interestingly, the characteristics of a good team member are also the characteristics of a good project manager. The team will reflect the leader who formed the team.

Don't forget that the project manager is also a member of the team. The project manager will have to look for people with complementary strengths, people who bring skills that the project manager might lack. Team assignments should include backups for key roles, including that of project manager. This calls for some duplication of skills, as well as meeting the fundamental objective of obtaining team members with complementary skills. Also, project managers must set an example through their own actions, demonstrating behavior consistent with the statements and policies they expect others to follow. A particular job for project managers is to run political interference for team members, to free them from bureaucratic constraints to enable them to do their jobs. The team leader, to use an analogy, has to be the lightning rod for the team.

Manager Alert

Project managers must set an example through their own actions, demonstrating behavior consistent with the statements and policies they expect others to follow.

Set Team Rules

Perhaps the best first step in establishing a project team is to develop clear rules of engagement for the team. The "ground rules" of the project should support an effective project environment. Effective projects maintain a culture of their own, and these rules will help create a project culture quickly. Sample ground rules include the following:

- Everyone has an equal opportunity to influence the final outcome. The project manager must protect the "playing field" with this rule of engagement. The culture and progress of the project depend on honest, vigorous debate. This rule of engagement does not mean that everyone has an equal vote, but that all participants should enthusiastically participate in the process. Team member roles will determine who gets to vote on particular matters.

- Issues get resolved through predefined channels. Issue resolution is most often ignored on projects because issues tend to cause discomfort. Effective issue resolution requires an established escalation process. This rule is intended to foster team cohesion and growth though effective communication and not meant to emphasize the "chain of command."

- Individuals are accountable. Projects are premised on people following through on commitments. Team members must clearly understand that they are accountable for results and their own participation.

- Team members listen to each other. Projects are energetic places, where new ideas and innovations are debated every day. In this exciting atmosphere, it is easy to adopt your own line of thinking and stop hearing the other ideas in the room. Effective project managers and stakeholders maintain the humility of listening first.

Define Roles and Responsibilities

Providing clear definitions of team members' roles and responsibilities, even generic definitions, establishes a framework for the project manager to set expectations and to foster teamwork and team building. The roles included on a given project team and the number of people filling those roles depend on a number of project variables, including size, scope, complexity, and budget. Project managers on larger efforts may consider commissioning a project "core team" composed of team members representing key task or functional roles. Members of the core team form the standing group that works most directly for and with the project manager.

Common roles on projects include the following, all or some of which may serve on a core team:

- *Executive sponsor.* This is a critical role on any project. The executive sponsor must provide leadership in support of the project's vision and goals. The executive sponsor needs to actively and visibly promote the project, obtaining the resources required and removing obstacles to successfully achieving the project objectives. A project with multiple sponsors may establish an advisory board comprising executives from organizations with a significant stake in the project's outcome.

- *Project director.* On larger projects, the project director may perform some of the responsibilities usually performed by the executive sponsor. In organizations where the executive sponsor supports many projects, the project director is the conduit for communication, status, and issue escalation between the sponsor and the project manager.

- *Project manager.* In the context of the core team, the project manager may need to play the role of facilitator, serving in an impartial role in core team meetings and other stakeholder interactions.

- *Business expert.* The primary responsibility of the business expert is to make sure that the organization's business interests are appropriately represented. The business expert typically serves as the translator between the business' interest and any technology-based project products or outcomes. Depending on the scale and scope of the project, the team may include one or more business experts. This core team member actively participates in the design and development of the project's outcomes, whether they are processes, policies, programs, or technology. The business expert is also often responsible for protecting or projecting the interests of the project's ultimate customers.

- *IT expert.* The IT expert on the project core team provides insight into the options and risks associated with possible technological solutions. Effective IT experts are able to translate technical issues and risks into plain English for the project manager, project team, and key stakeholders. For projects with IT vendors, the IT expert represents the government's interests and provides independent and objective evaluation and validation of each vendor's deliverables and final product.

- *Financial/budget expert.* Often overlooked on the project core teams, the financial/budget expert can provide the project manager and executive sponsor critical analysis of financial data, tracking actual costs against the budget. Early in the project's life, this team member can provide the financial justifications as part of the business case. The financial expert can also provide an early warning of cost overruns and determine impacts and "what-ifs" related to possible cuts to the project budget.

- *Contract specialist.* The growing emphasis in the federal government on acquisition and contract management makes the contract specialist a potential key player on a project core team and an important asset to the project manager. This role can include evaluating vendor performance and tracking compliance with contract terms and conditions, alerting the project manager to any deficiencies before minor issues become front-page news.

- *Subject matter experts* (SMEs). Throughout the life of any project, experts from a wide array of specialties may be needed. Their tenure on the project may be only as long as it takes to answer a specific question or, if they represent a unique specialty that is required for the project, the entire project lifecycle. The project manager should work with the business and IT experts to identify the need for SMEs as early in the project as possible so these experts will be available when needed.

DEVELOPING THE PROJECT TEAM

Teams, like people, go through various growth stages. The manager has to take the stages of team development and the needs of individual members into account when forming the team. Bruce Tuckman's seminal group theory identifies those stages as forming, storming, norming, performing, and adjourning.[9] Well known for its simplicity, this theory has been taught widely in project management (and human resource development) courses since it was first set forth over 40 years ago.

Table 3-1 describes actions and behaviors of the project manager and team members across the various project and team development phases. Suggested project manager actions for successfully developing a team are highlighted.

In fostering the team's development, the project manager should keep in mind three facets of members' needs: physical, professional, and personal. Simply stated, the team members should have an appropriate physical space conducive to work effectively and the necessary tools to do their jobs. In the case of virtual teams, the project manager should make sure that the critical technology is in place and is working to support the team's efforts across geographical areas and time zones.

Professional growth on the job is a key facet of an individual's full participation on a team. Challenging and interesting work, with commensurate support and training, will motivate team members and return dividends to the project in terms of greater commitment and loyalty to the project and higher-quality results. The personal facet refers to the project manager's responsibility to support each team member's job satisfaction and to foster a positive team environment.

TABLE 3-1
Stages of Team Development

Project Phase and Key Management Tasks	Team Stages and Team Behaviors	PM Actions
Initiation – Project manager identifies, selects, or recruits team members and defines roles and responsibilities.	*Forming* – Team defines purpose, composition, leadership patterns, and life span.	*Implement Structure* – Organize and direct work, and define team members' roles and responsibilities; get them off to an efficient start.
Planning – Project manager and team collaborate on developing key project management deliverables and establishing the appropriate project framework.	*Storming* – Team members experience "natural" conflict and tension as they work to establish and understand their roles.	*Coach* – Set high standards and clarify expectations, working collaboratively with the team; coach individuals on team participation.
Early Implementation – Negotiate changes and refinements to the project plan; develop project details.	*Norming* – Team members achieve greater levels of openness, trust, and confidence in each other and the group's ability to succeed.	*Encourage "Ownership"* – Empower team members to structure work and find ways to collaborate and solve problems independent from the project manager.
Implementation – Execution of project plan begins. Project manager's role shifts toward coordinating and integrating the project tasks.	*Performing* – Team has "matured" and is operating efficiently; project execution is smooth. In some cases, teams will achieve the status of "high performing" by becoming self-managing and self-motivating.	*Delegate, Coordinate, and Integrate* – Assign task responsibilities and ownership. Coordinate subteam activities and integrate project with internal and external elements.
Closeout – Project manager performs administrative wrap-up of the project. Assists or manages the reassignment of team members, as appropriate.	*Adjourning* – Team is anxious over the end of project and the uncertainty of next assignments.	*Coaching* – Conduct formal project closure for the group, celebrating success. Provide feedback on team members' performance and promote next project.

> **Manager Alert**
>
> Challenging and interesting work, with commensurate support and training, will motivate team members and return dividends to the project.

MANAGING THE PROJECT TEAM

Specific methods for managing project teams will be driven by the unique circumstances of the project. Methods are important, but they are secondary to basic leadership, management, and communications principles. Two key aspects of managing a project team are initiating the team and responding when the team runs into trouble. Knowing when a team isn't performing optimally or is regressing to a previous developmental stage is a critical skill for the project manager, as is seeking help before the situation deteriorates.

WORKING WITH CONTRACTORS

Project managers in the federal government often have to manage or work with outside contractors. The project manager must understand the contract as it relates to the project, particularly the timing and quality of deliverables. The project manager also has to keep in mind that contractors are from the private sector, where they may be accustomed to working in less procedurally restrained environments. In most cases, project managers will be able to rely on their organization's contract specialists or, if their project is large enough, team members with contract management responsibilities, to be the primary interface with contractor personnel (e.g., contracting officer's technical representative, or COTR). To the degree the project manager can focus on results rather than procedures, this will ease working with outside contractors.

CHARACTERISTICS OF SUCCESSFUL TEAMS

A strong project team is the foundation of most successful projects. Selecting the right team structure provides the appropriate framework for the team to form and effectively execute the project. Employing integrated project teams and virtual teams, both growing trends in the federal government, can provide project managers an effective structure for larger, more complex projects. Project managers who recognize the importance of the team and foster an effective group dynamic as well as each team member's individual goals will see dividends for their efforts in the form of loyalty and commitment.

Although every team has its own way of operating, successful teams seem to share ten key characteristics:

1. *Clearly defined project goals.* Clear goals enable team members to understand why they are doing their tasks and provide meaning to their work. Clear goals also help team members ensure that their work is meeting the project's ultimate goals and enable them to make any needed corrections without always having to consult with the project leader.

2. *Clearly defined roles.* Clearly defined roles enable team members to meet their responsibilities. When team members know what is expected of them and they are able to meet responsibilities, they will have opportunities for growth and expanded responsibilities.

3. *Open and clear communication.* Clear communication is essential at all stages of the project. The team needs to remain informed. The leader needs information to monitor progress and make any necessary adjustments, as well as to convey information to upper management and other stakeholders.

4. *Effective decision-making.* Decisions should be based on as much current information as possible, using a variety of methods.

5. *Balanced participation.* All team members participate in and contribute to the work of the team, not just their own tasks. The leader needs to encourage such balanced participation.

6. *Valued diversity.* Team members are valued for what they can uniquely bring to the team.

7. *Managed conflict.* Diversity of opinions is also important to a project team. Managed conflict means that different options are discussed and the best solution is arrived at— whether it is a compromise or a particular viewpoint. Managed conflict also means that problems are addressed, not avoided.

8. *Positive environment.* The feeling that each member of the team is valued and has something to contribute creates a positive environment. This climate of trust among members of the team, including the project manager, is critical to project success. Team members need to know that their colleagues can be depended on to do their jobs—that they are both willing and able.

9. *Cooperative relations.* A team is more than just a collection of individuals. Team members have to be willing to work with each other.

10. *Participative leaders.* The leader shares responsibility and glory when things work out—and takes the heat when things don't.

The more these characteristics are present, the greater the opportunity to build and maintain a successful project team.

NOTES

1. "Integrated Project Teams Guide for Use with DOE O 413.3A," U.S. Department of Energy, Washington, DC, September 24, 2008, pp. 1–2.

2. "Integrated Project Teams Guide for Use with DOE O 413.3A."

3. Office of Engineering and Construction Management, U.S. Department of Energy, Project Management Practices, Rev E, June 2003, Integrated Project Teams, Office of Management, Budget and Evaluation.

4. Ibid.

5. David I. Cleland and Lewis R. Ireland, *Project Management: Strategic Design and Implementation* (New York: McGraw-Hill, 2008), p. 427.

6. Deborah L. Duarte and Nancy Tennant Snyder, *Virtual Team Critical Success Factors* (Hoboken, NJ: John Wiley & Sons, 2003) pp. 289–290.

7. Terrence L. Gargiulo, "The Top Ten Strategies for Managers of Mobile Workers: Surviving and Thriving in the Emerging Mobile Workforce," Makingstories.net, www.scribd.com/doc/8958995/THE-TOP-TEN-STRATEGIES-FOR-MANAGERS-OF-MOBILE-WORKERS-Surviving-and-Thriving-in-the-Emerging-Mobile-Workforce (accessed April 2013).

8. "Teamwork," Answers.com, 2009, www.answers.com/topic/teamwork (accessed April 2013).

9. Bruce W. Tuckman, "Developmental sequence in small groups," *Psychological Bulletin* 63, 384–399. Reprinted in *Group Facilitation: A Research and Applications Journal*, Number 3, Spring 2001.

Chapter 4

LEVERAGING TECHNOLOGY FOR PROJECT SUCCESS

Information is the Currency for Democracy.

—THOMAS JEFFERSON

The federal government is utterly reliant on information technology to execute projects and programs of all shapes and sizes—from deep-sea exploration to GIS satellites and everything in between. Of the $80 billion the government spent on IT in 2012, a relatively small portion was for systems that support managing projects. These project management systems range from simple project scheduling applications to function-specific tools (like risk management) to portfolio management systems to full-fledged enterprise project management information systems. Government agencies rely heavily on these tools and systems throughout all phases of the project lifecycle.

Since 2009, the federal government has stepped up its oversight of information technology by strengthening the role of the federal CIO. The major challenges facing the federal CIO include mobile device management, cloud computing, big data, large IT projects, data centers, and broadband. These challenges have a direct impact on federal agencies and their current projects. Project management also relies increasingly on a wide range of systems, data feeds, and information channels, all of which contribute to a highly complex environment. From EVM data fields to the data required by E-300, a tremendous amount of source data is needed to adequately address the complexities of a modern project. Today's systems link directly into budgeting, human resources, information security, and other internal sources. Systems must extend beyond the firewall as well.

Federal and vendor-managed systems are more interrelated than ever. For example, the typical contractor EVM system must allow for federal access, reporting, and auditing. Project management systems must account for integrated governance processes, distributed teams, cross-border currency exchanges, and automated risk analysis. The project management software marketplace is as active as it ever has been. Commercial software is integrating more features into systems such as risk management, links to agency budgets, and automated E-300 submission to be responsive to the needs of the federal market.

INFORMATION TECHNOLOGY IN THE FEDERAL ENVIRONMENT

The federal government is undergoing significant changes in how it plans and deploys technology. Agencies are working to leverage single applications of technology across multiple organizations or functions. The concepts of reuse and scaling of technical platforms to accomplish project objectives are transforming both IT and non-IT projects. Project management systems must similarly scale up to integrate across and beyond project boundaries.

Manager Alert

Project management systems must scale up to integrate across and beyond project boundaries and should reflect the organization's capabilities and capacity for the discipline.

The evolution in technology is enabling government projects to reach beyond the typical set of stakeholders. Consider this example: Less than a month into his first term, President Barack Obama signed into law the American Recovery and Reinvestment Act of 2009 (ARRA), the largest public spending measure ever undertaken by the U.S. government. The law promised to create three to four million new jobs, refurbish our nation's public school facilities, overhaul the transportation infrastructure, make leaps in healthcare recordkeeping, increase college affordability, and develop a renewable energy infrastructure. ARRA promised to deliver funds to state and local governments to spur innovation and economic growth through public works projects. In typical Obama style, the President promised complete transparency of the spending through a website called "recovery.gov."

With nearly half the funds in the stimulus bill being administered by nonfederal entities,[1] the need for oversight and accountability was clear. Less than a year later, the White House rolled out a website designed to track ARRA dollars at work across the country. The site provides information from a variety of perspectives:

investments, opportunities, tracking and oversight, and impact. In addition, www.
data.gov delivers data feeds from a wide variety of government sources in easy-to-
navigate formats, fulfilling the promise of the President's open government initiative.

ASSESSING PROJECT NEEDS

Agencies need to balance their current project management requirements with
their aspirations for the next generation of project management in selecting IT
tools. Project management should begin with a set of business requirements and
processes from which tool use is derived and shaped. The agency's level of project
management maturity should guide the acquisition of a new tool.

Projects, like any other major organizational activity, have embedded business
functions that drive the need for technology. Project management has four major
functions: planning, executing, measuring, and reporting. Two of the functions—
planning and executing—are time-phased: Planning happens earlier; executing
happens later. (To be clear, this examination is focused on functions, not the phases
of a project lifecycle. A function fulfills a basic business need, whereas a project
phase is a time-bound set of activities.) The remaining two functions—measuring
and reporting—occur across all phases of a project.

Within each function, certain technologies must be used if the function is
to be fully realized. Technology's role is to support the execution and scaling of
those business functions. Figure 4-1 maps the project management applications or
technologies that support each function.

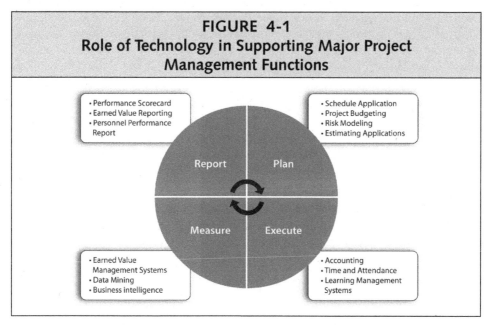

FIGURE 4-1
**Role of Technology in Supporting Major Project
Management Functions**

- Performance Scorecard
- Earned Value Reporting
- Personnel Performance
  Report

- Schedule Application
- Project Budgeting
- Risk Modeling
- Estimating Applications

Report   Plan

Measure   Execute

- Earned Value
  Management Systems
- Data Mining
- Business intelligence

- Accounting
- Time and Attendance
- Learning Management
  Systems

Planning

In the definition phase of a project, more is unknown than known. Early planning efforts are usually formed through basic word processing. Planning is also supported with scheduling applications, as well as budgeting and risk applications. In engineering and construction-oriented organizations, formal estimating software may be used in the planning stages. Many agencies engage in common preplanning activities, such as developing charters and scope statements. These types of project deliverables often follow templates.

As the work breakdown structure (WBS) is developed, the team needs to understand which tools will support the progression of this information from a WBS into the schedule. Early WBS information may also be incorporated into a solution in the discovery stage. Initial schedules are formed using scheduling software, and budgets are developed in spreadsheets or in agency-approved accounting software.

Executing

As projects move into execution, more transactional data (including materials use, time and attendance, and inventory tracking) need to be captured. Because execution is the most frenetic project phase, systems should be uploaded and ready to go. Some systems offer a robust, government-centric application that can track project requirements, schedule, cost, scope, and earned value.

Often, projects require more specialized tools that work in concert with the particular line of business. For example, GSA's Public Buildings Service uses an automated workflow system for its construction project management. This system helps GSA work with its numerous vendors more effectively and efficiently. Contractors can submit plans and revisions directly into the system, reducing paperwork significantly. As project documents are drafted, reviewed, finalized, and released, the system tracks these events and ensures that the documents follow predefined workflows.

Measuring

Measurement incorporates data gathering, analysis, and evaluation. Performance data (including EVM and non-EVM data such as contract milestones) are processed and displayed against performance baseline data. Typically, the measurement is a processing-intensive effort, and the output is only as good as the data going in.

Systems that measure need to directly access meaningful data, such as time and attendance data, schedule and EVM data, and financial data. On large projects, measurement can involve a staff of IT professionals.

Reporting

Reporting plays an important part in communicating the status of projects. Projects also play an important part in an agency's reporting. Technology that can deliver fast, accurate reports across large, complex projects is finally coming of age.

The George W. Bush administration used a scorecard approach to report on projects across the entire federal government. These scorecards had limited depth of information but provided a quick reference to the status of various initiatives. Under Obama, a host of new tools are available that have increased tracking of how government uses federal dollars with websites such as Recovery.gov, USASpending. gov, and the IT dashboard. Another website, Performance.gov, provides charts and graphs associated with agency spending on projects and programs. The underlying data are provided by project management and accounting systems, such as earned value reporting and budget appropriations.

Another example is E-300. OMB now requires that all agencies post their E-300s on their websites. While previously preparing an E-300 may have been a paperwork exercise that was limited to bureaucratic reviews, today's E-300s are free and open to the public, driving new levels of accountability in the reports.

TECHNOLOGY TRENDS IN PROJECT MANAGEMENT

New software being developed for project management in the federal government includes recordkeeping and access, accounting, website, and document-sharing programs. The project manager need not be an expert in these systems but should have a handle on their basic capabilities. Some of the new tools being developed are driving a new age of project information. Effective communication is key for the project manager.

Manager Alert

Many new technologies focus not only on getting the information into the tool but also on making the data accessible to a variety of audiences.

The following are three examples of new project technologies in the federal environment:

- *Predictive project management.* Newer project management solutions deliver a predictive project management capability to enhance the task-estimating process. This type of software tracks planned and actual time spent on tasks and uses the data to build estimates. Some vendors build estimates using thousands of data points from all their customers. So when an individual inputs a task called "conduct kickoff meeting," the tool can find other instances of kickoff meetings and estimate the time required.

- *Process-oriented project management.* As methodologies mature, agencies are struggling with how to integrate various lifecycles into one project. New process-oriented tools provide a robust interface that focuses on managing the process and workflow associated with project management.

- *Hosted solutions.* Most project solutions now offer a web interface. These solutions allow project teams to connect from anywhere, enter task information, retrieve reports, and more. In some instances, these solutions can be cheaper than a server-based option; however, security concerns may render a hosted solution infeasible unless it is hosted within the firewall.

Hundreds of project management packages are available in the marketplace today. Agencies should spend the time to gather and evaluate their requirements thoroughly before investing in any one system. Understanding current project management needs and capabilities, as well as the organization's direction, will help agency leadership invest in the right set of tools going forward.

Recovery.gov and data.gov are emblematic of the government's embracing new ways to reach out to citizens. In projects, similar technologies and approaches are being used to communicate with and manage project stakeholders. Used properly, technology can prove invaluable to government. Technology can make it easier for citizens to participate in government. It can enable them to use the government services they need efficiently and thereby get fuller value from their tax dollars. A good experience may encourage citizens to become better informed about the working of their government at all levels.

Technology is a tool designed to serve the project manager and project team. The particular circumstances of a project will call for a balance between locating and obtaining appropriate new technologies and making the best use of available technologies. The effectiveness of the selected hardware and software technologies will need to be monitored just as the entire project is monitored.

Manager Alert

The project manager and team will need to make adjustments to technologies used on the project as necessary.

Particularly useful emerging technologies are recordkeeping and access technologies, which will enable project managers to take advantage of institutional memory, culling lessons learned from past projects and storing them for the future benefit of new project managers. Used appropriately, technology is a tool that will enable government project managers to better serve the public.

NOTE

1. GAO Report 09-580, "As Initial Implementation Unfolds in States and Localities, Continued Attention to Accountability Issues Is Essential," April 2009.

Chapter 5

THE CRUCIAL ROLE OF COMMUNICATION

> *The speed of communications is wondrous to behold. It is also true that speed can multiply the distribution of information that we know to be untrue.*
>
> —EDWARD R. MORROW

On April 7, 1865, two days before the American Civil War ended, Abraham Lincoln sent a telegram to his commanding general, Ulysses S. Grant. The telegram read, "Gen. Sheridan says 'If the thing is pressed I think that Lee will surrender.' Let the thing be pressed."[1] This is a masterful example of concise communication. Lincoln—upper management—conveyed to his project manager, Grant, exactly what he wanted done. He also conveyed his reason, even though Grant likely knew that Lee and his formerly fearsome army had been forced to flee their Petersburg and Richmond defenses and should be caught. Two days after Grant received Lincoln's message, Lee surrendered.

Project managers are not likely to have their communications studied a century and a half after they are made. Project managers will also not likely be working for the same high stakes that Lincoln and Grant were. However, even seemingly small projects aimed at solving more mundane problems may well serve to prevent major future problems. As Lincoln showed in the entire body of his Civil War communication, "telling the story," or setting the project in context, is an important contributor—perhaps the most important contributor—to project success. This remains true today.

THE PROJECT MANAGER'S ROLE IN COMMUNICATION

"Ninety percent of a project manager's time is spent communicating" is a common maxim in the project management realm. How can this be? When you think about the complexity of communications in terms of content and channels (or paths), this scenario begins to make sense. PMI's *A Guide to the Project Management Body of Knowledge (PMBOK® Guide)* uses the formula *n(n-1)/2* to determine the total number of potential channels, where *"n"* represents the number of stakeholders. So if your "small" project has 20 team members, the executive stakeholders number about five, and three project managers from other divisions are interested in your progress, your project has 378 potential communication channels [28(28-1)/2 = 378]. As the *PMBOK® Guide* suggests, "a key component of planning the project's actual communications is to determine and limit who will communicate with whom and who will receive what information."[2]

Manager Alert

Communication is essential to secure buy-in from stakeholders throughout a project's life.

The project manager is typically the person responsible for selling the project vision, as well as the methods used to implement that vision. At the start of the project, the federal project manager should establish a communication program that reflects three basic purposes:

1.   *Disseminate and receive information*. The foundation of the communication program is a plan for what will be communicated, how, by whom, and to whom. Just as important is what information the project manager or team expects or needs to receive from stakeholders.

2.   *Achieve support for the project*. The project manager and team should use the content and context of the messages communicated to build and maintain support for the project and its outcomes. People cannot support what they don't know about.

3.   *Comply with federal reporting requirements*. Project managers must be cognizant of reporting requirements internal to their organization, the larger department, or federal policy agencies such as OMB and EPA. Multijurisdictional projects may also require reporting to state and local or even international government authorities.

SETTING THE CONTEXT

The key to fulfilling the purpose of communication is context. Why is context important? Try to identify the two missing numbers: <u>0</u> <u>7</u> <u>0</u> <u>4</u> <u>1</u> <u>7</u> _ _. Some people immediately try to figure a mathematical solution, while others try to discern a pattern. However, if additional information is provided, for example "American history," it becomes easier to determine that <u>7</u> and <u>6</u> are the last two numbers, completing the date the Declaration of Independence was signed.

Communication is all about context. The message must be relevant to the circumstance or framework within which it is received. The project leader has to be able to explain the context of the project; how the project fits into organization, agency, or department plans and goals; and how it meets the needs of the stakeholders. The appropriate context means that the message is delivered using the language, vocabulary, or common lexicon of the audience.

For a project with a wide variety of stakeholders, the project manager has the added complexity of communicating in a context that is appropriate for each distinct group. Although the audience and the context may vary, consistency in the message is critical to the credibility of the message and the messenger. Successful communication can be defined as getting the right message to the right people at the right time, using the right delivery methods and the right language.

Effective communication enables the project manager to maintain support throughout the project, particularly in the (likely) event that things do not go exactly as planned. The two-way aspects of communication give the project leader the information needed to detect and solve problems early, and to recognize and keep doing what is going well. Moreover, continuing open communication helps buy the project manager time to solve problems when they occur.

Manager Alert

Rule of thumb: Projects are 90 percent communication. Managers should expect a higher level of communication on projects.

COMMUNICATION MATRIX AND PLAN

Communication can be internal or external, with gradients and inter-connections (see Figure 5-1). Agency upper management, for example, can be considered either an internal or an external audience. Media is external, while customers might be considered internal or external. Communication can also be formal or informal. For example:

- *Formal external communications:* OMB Exhibit 300 (about as formal as a government report can get), Freedom of Information Act (FOIA) requests, and requests from Congress.

- *Formal internal communications:* Memoranda, budget exhibits, status reports, project presentations, and scope statements.

- *Informal external communications:* Phone calls from citizens or other agencies, e-mail inquiries, and news reports and articles.

- *Informal internal communications:* "Water cooler" meetings, e-mails, and even the project manager's behavior (which sets an example for team members).

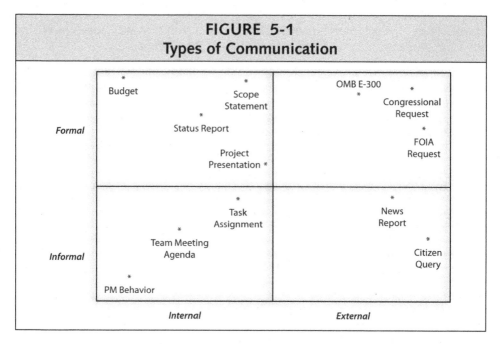

FIGURE 5-1
Types of Communication

A budget is usually a formal internal communication, occasionally shared formally or informally with external recipients. By comparison, Freedom of Information Act (FOIA) requests and citizen queries are always external, with the latter varying in formality. The relationship among internal/external and informal/formal is important because it indicates the level of effort required to develop, review, and disseminate the message, as well as the message itself and the communication method.

Finally, communication can be verbal or in writing. The most appropriate form of communication (e.g., e-mail, phone call, report) should be chosen for each audience. Even though communication should be tailored to the audience, the project manager should be careful not to deliver an inconsistent message by telling different audiences different things (or different versions of the same thing). Tailoring the context and message for audiences still requires consistency in content and intent.

Knowing the formality, source, and destination of various communications helps project managers allocate time and attention appropriately. Thus, the development and implementation of a formal communication plan is a critical tool. Project managers might create a matrix for each form of communication, including the following key elements:

- *Information need/message.* Description or outline of the specific information (e.g., project status, specific risk, upcoming event) that is the focus of the communication. If feedback is required, describe what information is expected and how it will be gathered.

- *From.* The individuals who will be the source or signatory of the message or information.

- *To.* The stakeholder groups or individuals who will receive the message or information.

- *Delivery method/communication medium.* The communication tool (e.g., e-mail, report, broadcast) or activity (e.g., meeting, demonstration, training) used to deliver the message or information.

- *Frequency/delivery date.* Timing of the contact (e.g., one time, weekly, monthly) and the delivery date.

- *Prepared by.* The person responsible for preparing the message (not necessarily the person named in "From"). This category may also identify the person required to approve the message or information to be disseminated.

The communication plan should be as detailed and specific as possible, including the names of the stakeholders and others responsible for particular areas. Effective communication plans are developed using the results of a thorough stakeholder analysis.

No matter the format or the specific content, the key is that a structured, documented plan for project communication will continually pay dividends. A project communication plan will facilitate the engagement of all key stakeholders, actively engage team members, and ensure that important messages are delivered and information is shared.

Manager Alert

Effective project communications are different from day-to-day communications. The communications plan is an essential tool for project managers.

Since communication is an operational as well as an informational tool, receiving information on project progress will let leaders and managers move to correct minor problems before they become major problems. Regular reports also provide a good opportunity to seek further input from stakeholders. The project manager should ask them not just if they like how things are going, but how things might be improved. This is also the time to look for support networks outside the project team, perhaps those undertaking similar or complementary functions. Effective information channels can only benefit project management.

THE ROLE OF THE MEDIA

Failed projects apparently make good headlines. Communicating with the media is an issue for any federal project manager who is senior enough to have authority to talk with the media. It is hard to argue against openness. Maintaining good relations with the media, when things are going well and even when they are not, buys the benefit of the doubt. This approach may secure the project manager time to correct problems if things do go wrong. News reports of problems, legal or otherwise, are bad enough. But when they end with "refused to comment," whatever the reality, it looks like the project manager is trying to hide something. All too often, managers and leaders, including elected political leaders, have in fact been trying to hide something.

How to deal with the media should be planned at the start of the project and consistently implemented during the project. At the outset, project managers should consider the potential media interest in their project. If the project has high visibility and may garner press attention, project managers should work with department executives, the media office, and legal counsel to determine an appropriate approach. The results of discussions (e.g., plans for press releases, interviews, town hall meetings) with the internal players should be integrated into the project communication plan.

INFORMATION ACCESS AND SECURITY

Federal officials have two additional factors to consider in dealing with the flow of information: access and security. First, the Freedom of Information Act (enacted in 1966) requires that certain materials be made public. In 1996 the act was amended to facilitate "public access to information in an electronic format."[3]

As a practical matter, project managers should be aware of their organization's policies and procedures associated with FOIA requests. In most situations, the office responsible for the department's FOIA process will inform the project manager when a request warrants action. Project managers should also consider the potential for future FOIA requests when determining the type of information and the method for archiving it once the project is complete.

Second, national security concerns require that certain materials not be made public. In consultation with upper management (possibly including the FOIA, security, legal, and inspector general offices), the project manager will to have to decide what information, if any, needs to remain confidential throughout the project, what information will need to remain confidential during certain phases of the project but can later be released, and what information should be totally open. Confidential or "classified" information may include private information about citizens (e.g., Social Security numbers, tax data) as well as national security information. Every federal agency is staffed with experts who are fully knowledgeable about information security and classification; the project manager should call on their expertise in establishing appropriate and legally compliant information security policies and procedures for the project.

Manager Alert

Effective communication can save a troubled project while poor communication can threaten a project that is on the path to success.

Successful federal project managers will find that a significant portion of their job requires them to communicate—to executives, team members, the interested public, probing media, and even a concerned Congress. Increased access to information, both accurate and inaccurate, will only increase the pressure on project managers to keep the information flowing both to and from the project's stakeholders. Employing technology will address part of the challenge, specifically methods, timing, and frequency. But at the end of the day, the project manager must have a sound communication plan, an effective approach to developing messages, a clear process for obtaining feedback, and a deep understanding of the project's context from the stakeholders' perspectives.

NOTES

1. Abraham Lincoln to Ulysses S. Grant, April 7, 1865, *The Literary Works of Abraham Lincoln*, selected, with an introduction by Carl van Doren and with illustrations by John Steuart Curry (NewYork: The Heritage Press, 1942), p. 276.

2. Project Management Institute, *A Guide to the Project Management Body of Knowledge (PMBOK® Guide), Fifth Edition* (Newtown Square, PA: Project Management Institute, 2013), p. 292.

3. General Services Administration, *Your Right to Federal Records: Questions and Answers on the Freedom of Information Act and Privacy Act*, May 2006, p. i.

Chapter 6

LEADERSHIP AND THE PROJECT MANAGER

I believe the techniques and principles that work are timeless. It's all about collaborating with people, building trust and confidence, and making sure you take care of the followers. You also need to give them what they need to do their work well, solve problems, face reality, create opportunities and monitor risks.

— GENERAL COLIN POWELL (U.S. ARMY RETIRED)[1]

The harsh and cynical view, regretfully often fact-based, is that the difference between leadership and management is that leaders motivate people to follow while managers force people to follow. As well as being cynical, for good leaders and managers, this view is oversimplified. A team needs both leaders and managers, and they can—even should—be the same people.

People running organizations, from the small work team assigned a task to the entire U.S. government, need to act as both leaders and managers, with strong elements of facilitator and mentor thrown into the mix. These are different roles, but they are compatible and complementary—and essential. Today's federal project managers must expand their focus to include elements of both leadership and management.

Leaders on projects are known by many names, commonly project or executive sponsor and project director. More important than their title, however, is their role. In federal projects, the role of leadership often transcends titles, falling to individuals with longevity, experience, or particular expertise. A critical attribute on any project, leadership cuts to the heart of project success in the federal sector. Consider the term *federal project leadership*. Each word suggests a universe of experience, know-how, and education. Combined, these three words suggest a challenging, complex work environment.

> **Manager Alert**
>
> In federal projects, the role of leadership often transcends titles, falling to individuals with longevity, experience, or particular expertise.

Leadership is often distributed across large projects, forming pockets and divisions within stakeholder groups. Some leaders in the federal environment come equipped with budgets; others arrive with nothing more than a vision. Regardless, it is critical to establish and cement leadership early on in a project setting.[2]

LEADERSHIP IN A PROJECT CONTEXT

The role of leadership can be described as creating, conceptualizing, and articulating a vision, which is sometimes described as the "why" of the project. The scope of that vision will vary according to the project, its tasks, and the nature of the group involved. The project manager will likely have been given an overall goal, and perhaps some parameters regarding methodology. He or she may have had input into creation of the overall vision.

As the de facto project leader, the project manager will not just run the project but will represent the project to stakeholders outside the organization, to other levels within the organization, and to the team members. The project vision has to align with the goals and perspectives of the organization, including employees, and the stakeholders. Developing and promoting a vision must take into account the diversity of missions within federal departments and recognize that team members' "day jobs" may have different (even conflicting) objectives from those of the project.

The project manager is the primary person responsible for "selling" the project's vision—the necessary first step to getting stakeholders and team members to buy into the need for the project. This common analogy to sales takes on a literal meaning to some of the stakeholders of government projects, particularly taxpayers, whose money is funding the project. The economy continues its slow recovery and for the foreseeable future, taxpayers are likely to demand increased assurance that they are getting their money's worth.

> **Manager Alert**
>
> The project manager "sells" the project's vision—the necessary first step to getting stakeholders and team members to buy into the need for the project and its intended outcomes.

Project leaders cannot just instruct their team members to do their jobs. Unlike in the days of what might be called command management, when team members know and actively support the team's goals, they are not only more motivated to do their jobs but are also better equipped to do them. For example, when team members know the purpose behind instructions, they are better able to carry them out and are more likely to take the initiative to adjust those instructions appropriately when higher management is not available. This is a continuous process, with the team leader needing to constantly look after the team members as well as stakeholders.

Tending to team members' and stakeholders' needs is one way a project manager can demonstrate leadership. The team leader, in essence, has to be a lightning rod—taking the heat for team members. Situations that require leadership action can include the following:

- Resolving conflicts among team members or between project stakeholders fairly and professionally
- Running political interference for team members, freeing them from bureaucratic constraints and thereby enabling them to do their jobs effectively
- Raising and promoting concerns raised by team members and stakeholders to the project sponsor or the organization's executives
- Actively fighting the inevitable resource battles, showing your team that you're willing to go to the mat to secure the personnel or material the project needs to be successful.

Leaders must set an example by their own actions, demonstrating behavior consistent with statements and policies they expect others to follow. A leader has to walk the walk as well as talk the talk. And just as leadership includes being a mentor to team members, the leader should find a mentor to provide an outside and objective view.

BALANCING LEADERSHIP AND MANAGEMENT

In a government project setting, where dotted lines of responsibility prevail and roles are often unclear, the project manager must strike a balance between leadership and management. In this context, leadership means creating and adjusting the vision and management means executing projects and carrying out daily operations to achieve the vision. In an organization, executives are responsible for strategic, vision-oriented action; project managers lead teams to deliver projects and operational managers lead personnel to deliver services. In the project context, the project manager must perform both leadership and management tasks to be successful. The federal government is seeing an increase in the emphasis on the project manager as leader as well as a need to improve or expand the project manager's skills and capabilities.

In the current federal environment, the project manager must shift from the hierarchical, leader-follower model to leading the team to achieve goals by applying a mix of leadership and management skills: collaboration, negotiation, and decisiveness. Project managers need to serve in the roles of facilitator and mentor to their teams, as well as change leaders in their organizations.

Manager Alert

Project managers need to serve in the roles of facilitator and mentor to their teams, as well as change leaders in their organizations.

Facilitator

Perhaps to a surprising extent, leadership skills in the federal government focus on building consensus and creating pockets of support. Eliciting project support demands that project leaders step in front of stakeholders and facilitate the process.

Facilitating is an important project management skill. In this role, the leader/manager does what is needed to enable team members to act with skill, confidence, and efficiency for the sake of the project, the organization, and themselves. The facilitator both models and creates methods for ending conflict within the team and between the team and stakeholders. He or she also works to secure needed project resources. To carry out these facilitation functions, the manager must to be able to communicate, in writing and verbally, with clarity and efficiency.

Mentor

As a mentor, the team leader models appropriate organizational and professional behavior for team members. He or she helps team members identify possibilities for problem solving and career path development. As a mentor, the team leader should display genuine personal interest in each team member's performance and development. From a practical perspective, projects serve as an excellent proving ground for leadership and an effective opportunity to develop an organization's next generation of leaders.

Change Leader

Projects are about change, yielding a new or improved process, service, or product. Project managers in the federal government must be prepared to accept the additional mantle of change leader.

As project managers increasingly embrace their role as change leaders, they will need to adjust their actions. Table 6-1 compares key activities of change leaders and project managers across four key functions. Performing both "sets" of actions will increase the opportunity for project success and the project manager's credibility in the leadership role.

TABLE 6-1 Key Activities of Change Leaders and Project Managers[3]		
	Change Leader	**Project Manager**
Sponsor Engagement	• Prepare sponsors for their role in the change process. • Provide content for their activities and interactions. • Check for "bad" behavior and guide desired behavior.	• Codify sponsors' roles and responsibilities. • Establish a framework for engaging sponsors and executives. • Inform on progress and facilitate decision-making and issue resolution.
Communication	• Emphasize the "why" and the "personal" impact of the project. • Elicit, encourage, and address good behavior. • Provide conduit for participation in change.	• Emphasize the facts—who, what, when, and how. • Facilitate action, deliverables, and outcomes. • Provide conduit for information sharing.
Coaching and Training	• Build change management competency across key stakeholder groups. • Identify and train change agents. • Coach and guide sponsors and affected people through the change.	• Direct task managers and team members in executing project management processes. • Identify gaps to train on changes in core processes. • Provide structure for developing new technical skills to adopt change.
Resistance Management	• Prevent—build change management competency in the organization's leaders.	• React—build coping processes and competencies of sponsors, project managers, and key team members.

CHARACTERISTICS AND TRAITS OF PROJECT LEADERS

To be effective in their roles as facilitator, mentor, and change leader, project managers must exhibit certain key characteristics and traits. These include understanding (and demonstrating) the difference between authority and responsibility, displaying confidence, and recognizing and facing reality.

Authority vs. Responsibility

Authority and responsibility are related, but they are not the same. Authority means having the power to get a task done, whereas responsibility means having to accomplish a goal. Authority and responsibility are also related to the ability to get a task done. Authority without responsibility is useless. Responsibility without authority is equally useless, and far more frustrating.

Responsibility has another meaning. A project manager can assign an aspect of a project to a team member, giving that person authority to get the job done. The team member is then responsible to the project manager for getting the job done. The person doing the delegating remains responsible to his or her bosses for accomplishing the assigned task.

The project manager can delegate what might be called functional responsibility, but not ultimate responsibility. The leader/manager's role as facilitator involves obtaining the proper resources to enable the project staff to do their jobs. Appropriate authority to do the job is one of those resources. Any limits on authority, including spending, can affect the team member's ability to carry out the project. Subordinate task managers cannot be blamed if these limits hamper task success.

Manager Alert

The project manager can delegate functional responsibility, but not ultimate responsibility.

Confidence

Management coach and writer D. A. Benton has an interesting chapter title in her book *CEO Material: How to be a Leader in Any Organization*: "You Feel Broadly Adequate."[4] Her point is that a leader needs to demonstrate confidence in his or her ability to do the job, regardless of how the leader might actually feel. Benton offers some ways a leader can look at the record and find reasons to be confident. "Confidence is the driver behind everything. . . .People are drawn to you; they want to be around you, do like you, learn from you, and be highly thought of by you. People are happy to follow you because you are more fun to be around."[5]

Confidence also signals the leader's conviction that the job can and should be done. One way a leader expresses confidence is by enlisting others with skills in which the leader might not be as strong. For example, ideally the leader should also be a manager. But a realistic leader will have assessed, both formally and informally, his or her abilities and perhaps found less skill in, say, administration. An effective and confident leader will then select a number two person who is a good administrator.

Recognizing and Facing Reality

Referring to the person running a project as the "leader" or the "manager" is just convenient shorthand. The person running the project should actually be called the "leader/manager/facilitator/mentor." The leader has to be all four at once, calling up whatever skills are needed for the particular situation. As General Colin Powell noted, this ability starts with knowing and facing reality.

Some of the basic leadership functions, in particular regular interaction with stakeholders and staff members, can give the leader a crucial heads up in determining and recognizing reality—and any changes in reality. For example, facing reality may require a project manager to take the unpopular, but necessary step of informing executives that the project will be delayed or will exceed the budget. Particularly when the facts are uncomfortable or bad, facing reality is a prominent trait of leaders.

LEADING AND MANAGING PROJECTS IN THE FEDERAL GOVERNMENT

Leaders have to manage as much as managers have to lead. Successful management on the part of leaders (e.g., executives and sponsors in the project context) is seen in their willingness and ability to participate in relevant project management activities, remove barriers (e.g., organizational, political, resource), and support the development of their project managers.

Project managers in the federal government face all the demands and realities that project managers in the private sector face, including (especially in the current economic environment) responsibility for the bottom line: delivering projects on budget and on time. The ARRA raised the bar on both leadership and management by federal government project managers and continues to affect how projects are managed. The ARRA funds allocated to projects came with requirements for new or expanded management controls and increased reporting, requiring project managers to demonstrate that their projects are returning value for the money spent. This is a clear example of the demand on federal project managers to lead as well as manage. Project managers must give their subordinates the resources needed to carry out assigned tasks, along with the authority (with any limits clearly stated) to do their jobs.

Federal government project managers face at least one more challenge than project managers in the private sector do. They have a far larger number of outside stakeholders: the entire tax-paying population of the United States. The federal government does not just have to work effectively and efficiently, but it also has to be perceived as working effectively and efficiently. Trust in the government's ability, dedication, and honesty is nothing short of critical in today's environment.

Manager Alert

A federal project manager is at the front lines of demonstrating the value of government and combating perceptions of government inefficiency.

THE CHALLENGE FOR FEDERAL MANAGERS

The challenge for federal project managers starts with the continuously evolving view of the role of the federal government, along a spectrum from "the source of all problems" to "the solution to all problems." In reaction to the major financial crisis that began in 2008, the idea of a federal government actively involved in monitoring the private sector has gained far more support than it had just a few years ago. The public is demanding not just that the government do more—this pendulum will likely swing back—but that it do what it does better. That is not likely to change.

An issue within the government is that there are really two types of government employees, career civil servants and political appointees. The former are likely to be in government until retirement. The latter are in government, for the most, just during the time in office of the current administration. The civil servants are repositories of institutional memory. Political appointees tend to see themselves as agents of change.

In addition to exercising good management and leadership, political appointees can ameliorate this natural tension by recognizing and crediting the institutional memory and experience of career civil servants, rather than regarding them as hidebound bureaucrats. Equally, career federal employees should regard, and judge, political appointees as agents of refreshing change rather than as political hacks seeking change for the sake of change.

NOTES

1. "Lessons in Leadership," *PM Network*, vol. 22, issue 6, August 2008, p. 61.

2. Vijay K. Verma and R. Max Wideman, "Project Manager to Project Leader? and the Rocky Road Between..." rev. 3 (06-11-02), presented at PMI's 25th Annual Seminar and Symposium, Vancouver, BC, Canada, October 17, 1994.

3. Jonathan Weinstein and Tom Marsicano, "Change Management vs. Project Management: Who Should Lead," presentation at the Association of Change Management Professionals Africa Conference, November 5–7, 2012.

4. D.A. Benton, *CEO Material: How to Be a Leader in Any Organization* (New York: McGraw Hill, 2009), pp. 69–78.

5. Benton, p. 69.

Chapter 7

ENGAGING STAKEHOLDERS

> *. . . I have found no greater satisfaction than achieving success through honest dealing and strict adherence to the view that, for you to gain, those you deal with should gain as well.*
>
> —ALAN GREENSPAN, FORMER CHAIRMAN OF THE FEDERAL RESERVE[1]

In the 21st century world of work, the term *stakeholder management* is almost an oxymoron. In so many situations, stakeholders try to manage the managers. Stakeholders maintain a distinct advantage, with up-to-the-second communications, extensive media outlets, and instant links to diverse constituencies through collaborative websites. Information simply flows too fast for any project team to be able to control or even manage it. In most cases, the best a project manager can hope to do is stay abreast of the information and try to shape it toward a successful project conclusion. Nevertheless, project managers are often asked to do more than just keep up with the information.

Understanding the power, influence, and importance of the project's relationships with various stakeholders is key to obtaining and maintaining support, buy-in, and participation. In short, vigorous stakeholder management is critical to the success of a project.

WHO ARE THE STAKEHOLDERS IN FEDERAL PROJECTS?

Federal projects bring together diverse constituencies and powerful people. For federal project managers, getting stakeholders to believe in the project is a key, and challenging, success factor. The best project managers have a story to tell; for their project to be successful, stakeholders need to believe that story. The story could be about defending the nation from attack, cleaning up nuclear waste, or putting a space station into orbit. Federal projects serve the national interest, and stakeholder management should originate from that foundation.

Project managers must view stakeholder management as more than just a set of tasks to be accomplished, but rather as a channel for promoting the project. Stakeholders should understand why a project is important and the rationale behind the project approach and methodology. Federal project managers must be aware of stakeholders' interests and power to affect the project and to actively engage stakeholders throughout the project.

Manager Alert

Stakeholder management is more than just a set of tasks to be accomplished; it is a channel for the project manager to promote the project.

Internally, stakeholders include the project manager, customer, project team members, and sponsor, as well as the organization carrying out the project. In many projects, the most significant (and immediate) stakeholders are the relevant senior leaders and decision-makers in the organization. The level at which the project is performed (e.g., departmentwide or within a subordinate agency), as well as the project manager's chain of command, determines who the project's executive stakeholders are. Project managers should not forget that the agency's IG might be an important stakeholder as well. Stakeholder groups on federal projects include a wide range of constituents, from federal employees to local governments to industry groups (see Figure 7-1):

- *Congress.* As the ultimate stakeholder, Congress, through committees and oversight activities, has the power to fund, continue, increase, modify, or eliminate most federal government projects. A single large project may fall under the purview of one or several congressional committees.

- *The President and agency leaders.* Elected and appointed leaders often bring with them a specific agenda and have limited windows of opportunity for introducing change. If elected and appointed leaders fail to achieve the necessary buy-in and cooperation from civil servants, they may find that a project is implemented to its minimum requirements and is not "owned" by the stakeholders. Civil servants, on the other hand, provide continuity across administrations, legislative cycles, and priorities. Civil servant leaders have the power to resist change, knowing that time is on their side for any given mandate. This inherent difference in perspective between appointed leaders and civil servants could become either a strong catalyst for effective project management or a war of wills.

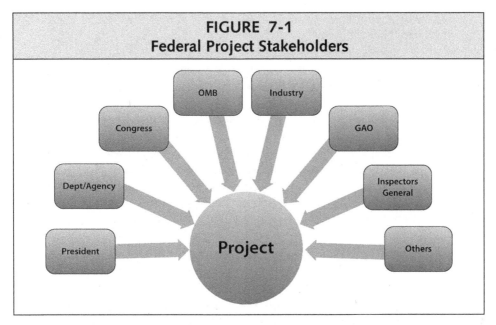

FIGURE 7-1
Federal Project Stakeholders

- *Office of Management and Budget.* OMB plays a leadership role in defining the priorities, policies, and direction of the executive branch. A variety of OMB's policies are directly related to the practice of project management in the federal government. As an interested stakeholder, OMB gains insight into major projects through E-300. Further, FAC-P/PM is the training framework OMB has established in its effort to improve project management in the federal government.

- *Government Accountability Office.* GAO is the investigative arm of Congress. Every two years since 1990, GAO has reported on high-risk areas to bring attention to opportunities for improving government performance. The "high risk" GAO identifies is commonly related to "vulnerabilities to fraud, waste, abuse, and mismanagement." Through GAO's work, a deep well of lessons learned has emerged, uncovering both the failures and successes of projects and programs across the federal government. Like OMB, GAO is an interested party in project performance. Projects executed by organizations on the high-risk list are clearly under more scrutiny. Furthermore, its government-wide view gives GAO status as a stakeholder in some projects.

- *Department and interagency stakeholders.* Perhaps the most common and direct stakeholders are the department staff involved in a project—whether as team members or as internal customers. Typically, these stakeholders have a significant vested interest in the outcome of the project, often as owners of the new processes, systems, tools, or products. Proactively managing and actively engaging this stakeholder group will likely yield the greatest benefit, ideally by gaining their enthusiastic support or at the very least by overcoming their resistance.

- *The public.* Although in theory the ultimate source of government power in a democracy lies with the people, the public often has very little visibility in federal projects. Through their representative bodies and public hearings, individuals and organizations may participate directly in project reviews as well as in lobbying efforts for and against particular projects and project alternatives.

- *Opposition stakeholders.* Although not found in every project, this is a special class of stakeholders who perceive themselves as being harmed if the project is successful. An example might be a community that opposes a new government facility being built. Early involvement of opposition stakeholders may result in a more positive outcome; conversely, neglecting these stakeholders can doom a project.

- *The media.* The media generally pay attention to major projects with large budgets. The press has a duty to report objectively but often focuses more on problems than successes.

- *Vendors/suppliers/industry.* In the procurement process, vendors and suppliers are often important stakeholders. Besides selling products or services, this stakeholder group puts its reputation and future business on the line with nearly every project. The tangled web of procurement policies and practices creates a complicated relationship between the companies that "play the game" of government contracting and the federal departments and agencies that execute the projects. Government project managers treat vendors at times as adversaries and at other times as partners. In each case they must be managed appropriately as stakeholders.

- *Future generations.* During its limited tenure, each administration has a responsibility to future generations regarding long-term debt, viable and affordable infrastructure, and a healthy environment. Interest groups that lobby for or against a project's outcomes often represent these stakeholders.

Effective stakeholder management in the federal sector begins with identification of the individuals, organizations, and markets that will have a bearing on the project. Working with these various, often disparate, groups requires skills that have emerged from the new age of information technology. Treating stakeholders like static entities that need the occasional information update is a mistake. Instead, stakeholders should be viewed as dynamic groups that form, congregate, and separate easily. The federal project manager should strive to build partnerships with stakeholder groups by understanding their concerns and goals related to the project, as well as through effective communication that invites their active participation in the appropriate elements of the project.

Manager Alert

The federal project manager should strive to build partnerships with stakeholder groups by understanding the project from their perspective—their concerns and goals.

MANAGING STAKEHOLDERS IN A COMPLEX ENVIRONMENT

Living in this complex world and engaging in multilayered, complicated federal projects means adopting a vigorous approach to managing stakeholders. Kathleen Hass, in her book *Managing Complex Projects: A New Model,* describes the following key elements.[2]

- *Establish positive relationships with key stakeholders.* Use stakeholder assessment and management techniques to help create a positive relationship with key stakeholders. In addition, build and maintain a direct one-on-one connection with the most critical stakeholders by calling (not e-mailing) them on a regular basis. Do not shy away from adversaries; engage them in constructive conversations in an effort to mitigate their influence or turn them into allies.[3]

- *Involve customers and users in every aspect of the project.* Avoid the urge to limit interaction with customers and users in the time between soliciting their needs and delivering the project results. Maintain their active participation throughout the project in order to uncover unexpected impacts or identify opportunities to improve the project results.

- *Establish and manage virtual alliances.* In the federal government, engage a variety of external stakeholders—political or interest groups, other agencies, suppliers, or industry—to form alliances and thereby provide support, help identify potential issues, or secure needed resources for the project.

- *Establish and manage expectations.* At the outset, as well as throughout the project, document, understand, and address expectations, including resolving unreasonable expectations. Without clearly establishing or managing stakeholders' expectations, a project manager is almost guaranteed to fail to satisfy them.

The most effective federal project managers develop an approach to stakeholder management that incorporates the nature of the team (collaborative, virtual, command and control, etc.). Projects tell stories, and the best people to tell them are the stakeholders—the people who have come to believe in the objectives of the project.

CONDUCTING A STAKEHOLDER ASSESSMENT

Increasing access to information and the growing number of sources complicates stakeholder management. Given the overabundance of information available today, project managers must assume that stakeholders believe they know as much, if not more, than the project team members. Lacking any real control over the flow of information, the project manager, sponsors, and team members must try to harness the forces that influence stakeholder behavior and attitudes.

An effective tool for managing stakeholder involvement in a federal project is the stakeholder assessment. A stakeholder assessment can be used to gauge the dimensions that drive stakeholder behavior, such as attitudes and biases toward the project, extent of influence over the project team members, aversion to conflict, and geographic factors. The assessment will provide important information that will help the project manager and team develop an approach to managing stakeholders effectively.

Stakeholder assessments can take a variety of forms and can involve various tools and methods. Simplicity and utility are the keys to performing the right level of analysis. The assessment should be simple to understand and execute, and should be designed to provide information that the project manager and team members can use to communicate effectively with stakeholders and achieve the shared project goals. Key elements of any stakeholder assessment should include the group (or individual), their concerns/issues/goals, a description of their influence/impact on the project, and actions to manage/engage them. A straightforward worksheet (see Table 7-1) will suit the needs of most projects.[4]

TABLE 7-1 Stakeholder Assessment Worksheet					
Stakeholders (Individuals or Groups)	Involvement/ Role	Priorities/ Concerns	Level of Support Needed	Current Level of Support	Influence Strategy
Department CIO	Resource supplier	Clear requirements, solution uses existing technology, user adoption	3 – Needs to promote project and secure needed resources	+	CIO is the chair of the project's advisory board. Keep CIO informed of status and any issues – "no surprises."

The following are definitions for the columns in the worksheet:

- *Stakeholders (individuals or groups)*: These individuals or groups include those requesting the project; those the project manager must go through for resources, approval, guidance, etc.; those who will use the product/service; and others who can influence the project.

- *Involvement/role*: Based on the stakeholder description, identify their role or involvement—sponsor, requester, owner, resource supplier, customer, or end-user.

- *Priorities/concerns*: What are the important or risky areas of this project from the stakeholder's perspective?

- *Level of support needed*: "1" = Their support is not necessary now; "2" = Helpful to have their support; and "3" = Critical to have their support.

- *Current level of support*: "+" = Actively supports the project; "0" = Neutral to the project; "−" = Opposes the project and may work against it; and "?" = Unknown level of support.

- *Influence strategy*: Methods for engaging and managing the stakeholder's participation on the project.

Another, more complex assessment tool, originally developed in the adult education arena, addresses the "influence" and "interest" relationships between stakeholders and the project (see Figure 7-2).[5] This tool guides project managers and team members in the tactics they can employ to manage relationships with their stakeholders.

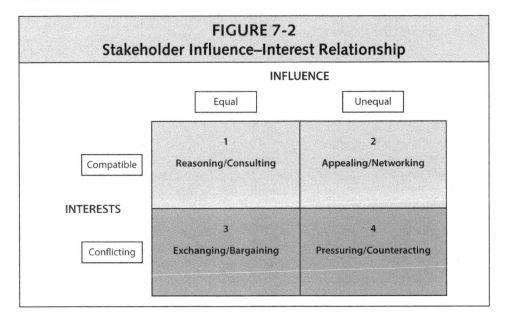

FIGURE 7-2
Stakeholder Influence–Interest Relationship

	INFLUENCE	
	Equal	Unequal
Compatible	**1** Reasoning/Consulting	**2** Appealing/Networking
INTERESTS Conflicting	**3** Exchanging/Bargaining	**4** Pressuring/Counteracting

Why use such an involved technique? For complex or politically charged projects (common in the federal government), a detailed stakeholder assessment can guide project leaders toward specific actions that will enable them to manage stakeholders more effectively. In addition, team members will gain a greater appreciation for the interests and concerns about the project from the stakeholders' perspectives. The project manager and team members will then be able to adjust their behavior, the information they provide, and the methods they use to communicate with each stakeholder accordingly.

Manager Alert

For complex or politically charged projects, a detailed stakeholder assessment can guide project leaders toward specific actions that will enable them to manage stakeholders more effectively and avoid conflicts.

Each quadrant in Figure 7-2 describes the techniques a project manager should employ depending on the extent of agreement or conflict between the project and each stakeholder (individually or as a group). For example, alignment of interests and influence allows the project manager to be more consultative or collaborative, while misalignment requires escalating levels of action on the part of the project manager—either more diplomacy or the engagement of other stakeholders to appeal or apply pressure as needed.[6] This approach enables the project manager to communicate effectively with stakeholders and provides the team the information needed to meet the stakeholders' expectations.

Stakeholders with influence equal to the project manager's and with compatible interests (cell 1) are important allies to a project. The project manager and team should maintain a good working relationship with these stakeholders; the communication plan should reflect methods for keeping them informed and supportive, and they should be encouraged to champion the project.

Stakeholders with unequal influence and compatible interests (cell 2) are allies of the project and should not require a high level of resources to enhance their relationship with the project; however, a project team member could be designated to address their needs. The project communication plan should include methods for keeping them informed.

Stakeholders with equal influence but conflicting interests (cell 3) may pose a limited risk to the project. The risk plan should include an item that addresses monitoring these stakeholders in case their level of influence changes. They should also be kept informed about project progress through general communications.

Stakeholders with unequal influence and conflicting interests (cell 4) may pose a significant risk to the project and therefore require active management throughout the project. The risk management plan should include a mitigation plan with regard to these stakeholders. The communication plan should include ways to keep them appropriately informed as well as ways to persuade them to take ownership and to gain their support. These stakeholders will need to be monitored closely. If these strategies fail, the project manager may be faced with giving in to their demands.

The result of the analysis can yield a better understanding of the relationships between stakeholders and the project manager, and can also improve the quality of interactions with each group. Above all, project managers and team members must remain focused on constructively engaging stakeholders as part of their efforts to achieve project goals and outcomes.

Manager Alert

Project managers and team members must remain focused on constructively engaging stakeholders as part of their efforts to achieve project goals and outcomes.

Today more than ever, it is important for project managers in the federal government to understand a project's relationship with executive stakeholders and the considerable power and influence they wield. Project managers can employ a structured stakeholder management approach and skills to lead the relationships with their stakeholders and maintain their support. Project managers must work closely with stakeholders, listening to their wants and needs and employing techniques to advance their support. This two-way communication is a key ingredient of effective project management.

NOTES

1. Remarks made May 13, 2004, before the Federal Reserve Bank of Chicago's Smart Money Conference, https://fraser.stlouisfed.org/historicaldocs/ag04/download/29216/Greenspan_20040513.pdf (accessed April 2013).

2. Kathleen B. Hass, *Managing Complex Projects: A New Model* (Vienna, VA: Management Concepts, 2009, pp. 219–224. Adapted with permission.

3. Brian Irwin, *Managing Politics and Conflict in Projects* (Vienna, VA: Management Concepts, 2008).

4. Hass, p. 218. Adapted with permission.

5. Ronald M. Cervero and Arthur L. Wilson, "The Politics of Responsibility: A Theory of Program Planning Practice for Adult Education." *Adult Education Quarterly* 45 (1) (Fall 1994): 261.

6. David I. Cleland and Lewis R. Ireland, *Project Management Handbook: Applying Best Practices Across Global Industries* (New York: McGraw Hill, 2008).

Chapter 8

PROJECT MANAGEMENT COMPETENCIES AND SKILLS

Our job as a federal agency is management and oversight, to be responsible stewards of the public's trust and resources. Therefore, we must have a highly qualified and technically proficient management team and staff. My aim is to have a high performing organization, sustained by a career oriented workforce, driven to produce results that are important now and into the future.

—JAMES A. RISPOLI, FORMER ASSISTANT SECRETARY, U.S. DEPARTMENT OF ENERGY[1]

The federal workforce is changing. Numerous surveys and assessments conducted by OMB, GAO, and individual agencies in cooperation with industry have shown that project management, and in particular the skills associated with being a successful project manager, are critical to agencies achieving their missions.[2] The practice and discipline of project management has been institutionalized on the defense side of the federal government for years. The Defense Acquisition University (DAU) and the Defense Acquisition Workforce Improvement Act (DAWIA) certification in a variety of project and program management-related areas are clear examples of this commitment to the development of project management skills and competencies. In the past few years, the practice and discipline of project management have been expanding by leaps and bounds across the civilian side of the federal government as well.

OMB and a growing number of agencies have recognized and begun to realize the benefits of a formal approach to building and maintaining project management competencies and skills as part of their goals to improve the quality and success rate of projects in the federal government. Nonetheless, recent studies indicate that formal training lags behind the increased demand for, and the responsibility and accountability of, project managers. A joint study commissioned by OMB and the Council for Excellence in Government, for example, found that up to half of the project managers surveyed had not received training in critical project management areas. Most who had received training rated it "moderately" to "highly" valuable.[3]

The emergence of project management as a core competency in the federal government signals a shift in the career paths and opportunities for government personnel. Agencies across the government are establishing programs to identify, train, and certify individuals as project managers. OMB has further confirmed the arrival of project management on the federal scene with the development and implementation of the federal acquisition certification for program and project managers (FAC-P/PM), which requires agencies to train and develop program and project managers. Agencies that have already started down the project management path are now working to comply with this standard, while others with less mature project management capability must build programs to meet the FAC-P/PM requirements.

Manager Alert

Federal agencies are responsible for implementing project manager certification that is compliant with FAC-P/PM.

WHAT ARE THE CRITICAL SKILLS?

Although the emphasis differs from agency to agency, most successful federal project managers share a fairly consistent set of skills. Project management in the federal government is moving beyond what are commonly thought of as "traditional" skills. Many organizations are focusing on a more comprehensive set of skills and competencies, including core project management skills, communication skills, emerging project management skills, and subject matter expertise. Table 8-1 compares the skills in these categories with traditional project management skills.

Every two years, the federal CIO Council updates the core competencies associated with the Clinger-Cohen Act. In addition to the core project management competencies, the list includes emerging competency areas like leadership, change management, and performance assessment that require skills not normally found in project managers who rise through the technology ranks in the federal government. The emphasis on these Clinger-Cohen competencies further suggests that successful federal project managers must expand their capabilities beyond their technical expertise.

TABLE 8-1
Comparison of Traditional and New Project Management Skills

Traditional Emphasis	Scheduling	Budgeting	Quality Management	Risk Management	Facilitation	Communication	Leadership	Business Writing	Management	Negotiation
New Emphasis										
Integration/Coordination					✓	✓		✓	✓	
Supervision	✓		✓		✓	✓	✓		✓	
Analysis	✓	✓		✓						
Contractor Management	✓	✓	✓	✓	✓	✓		✓	✓	
Lessons Learned/ Knowledge Management			✓	✓		✓		✓		
Negotiation	✓	✓		✓	✓	✓	✓		✓	
Teaching/Mentoring					✓	✓	✓	✓	✓	
Framing	✓	✓	✓	✓	✓	✓	✓	✓		✓
Messaging/Context					✓	✓	✓	✓	✓	
Integration						✓	✓			
Workflow						✓	✓	✓	✓	✓
Facilitation	✓	✓	✓	✓	✓	✓			✓	✓
Integrity	✓	✓	✓	✓		✓	✓		✓	✓

CORE PROJECT MANAGEMENT SKILLS

The core set of skills needed for success as a project manager in a federal agency derives from the primary knowledge areas described in PMI's *A Guide to the Project Management Body of Knowledge (PMBOK® Guide)*.[4]

Leadership

Government project managers are increasingly relied on to fill a leadership role in their organization. As the primary person responsible for the use of an agency's resources to achieve goals and introduce improvements to the organization, the project manager is increasingly being brought into the decision-making process to contribute to setting strategic direction, allocating resources, and defining goals.

The rising prominence of project managers (and project management overall) is evident in organizations where the PMO resides at the C-level (e.g., chief information officer, chief financial officer) in the organization. The PMO is actively involved in setting policy and providing guidance on executing projects.

Manager Alert

The PMO is increasingly being brought into the decision-making process to contribute to setting strategic direction, allocating resources, and defining goals.

Coordination

The increasing complexity of projects and the dispersion of tasks, resources, and stakeholders across organizations make coordination high on the list of key skills. The involvement of multiple stakeholders (federal, state, and local government representatives), execution of tasks across various disciplines (construction, contracting, security, real estate, and technology), and compliance with myriad regulations and standards make this skill critical to the effective execution of projects. Conducting formal project reviews at regular intervals, typically in conjunction with major project phases, can go a long way toward effective coordination on a project.

Supervision

Project management involves the supervision of resources to achieve the project's outcomes. Strong project management practices provide a solid structure that project managers can rely on to ensure that their team gets the right tasks done right. One common challenge is the lack of supervisory experience among people thrust into the project manager role. In many agencies, project managers rise through technical career paths and have little if any experience supervising a team. To develop in their new role, they require greater guidance and support as "new" supervisors.

Risk Assessment/Management

Effective risk analysis is key to successful project planning. The results of this analysis should trigger changes to project plans or baselines, as well as the development of mitigation plans. Any adjustments to the project plan, schedule, work breakdown schedule, or budget in response to the risk assessment should be documented and communicated, especially to the executive sponsor and any oversight or guiding organizations. These stakeholders should be made aware of necessary changes to the project and their potential impacts—and asked to approve those changes. Early information on risk minimizes surprises later in the project.

Project Analysis and Requirements Definition

The effort involved in project analysis and requirements definition (which involve an iterative process that goes deeper and deeper to get to exact project needs) is universally underestimated. Project managers need to be able to link good analysis—business, technical, and economic—with project communications, understanding and conveying requirements from the customer's perspective. Thorough planning should be conducted at the front end of the project, and all key stakeholders should vet the resulting plans.

Contractor Management

Managing contractors is a critical skill in agencies where outsourcing is prevalent. Successful project managers integrate contractor personnel fully into their project teams. The choice of contract type can assist in effective contractor management and thereby contribute to project success. Many agencies favor the use of cost-plus award or incentive fee (CPAF or CPIF) contracts, which promote efficient execution by contractors to meet established performance goals.

Stakeholder Management

Project managers must work within and across multiple groups of stakeholders who may control or influence funding, personnel, key resources, legislation or regulation, and decision-making authority.

Schedule, Scope, and Change Management

The criticality of the fundamental skills associated with managing the project schedule and scope is common across organizations and projects. In addition, throughout a project's lifecycle, the project manager must continuously identify, assess, and manage the impacts of changes, answering the question, "If this change occurs, what impact will it have on the project scope, schedule, budget, and requirements?" Formal change processes enable project managers to clearly communicate the facts of potential impacts to the relevant stakeholders, limiting the emotion associated with altering anticipated outcomes.

Lessons Learned

Although most organizations identify gathering lessons learned as a critical skill, few take the appropriate time to perform the function.

Manager Alert

Government managers would be well-advised to understand the skills and abilities required in a project setting. A line manager who understands projects is a project manager's best friend.

Financial Analysis and Budgeting

Frequent budgetary fluctuations increase the challenges of managing projects in the federal government. The fiscal crisis is compounding the ever-present stress on project managers to deliver projects with limited financial resources. The need to be efficient with taxpayers' money, particularly in the current fiscal environment, has increased the need for project managers to have strong financial analysis and budgeting skills. Among the key skills needed are the following:

- *Budget forecasting and financial projections.* At a minimum, project managers in the federal government should be adept at building a cost estimate that takes into consideration the budgetary and spending cycles and presents a "total ownership cost" figure.

- *Financial and economic analysis.* An understanding of the internal and external conditions that will influence the project is critical for project managers.

- *Budget control/cost management.* Project managers must be able to use tools and methodologies, such as earned value, that can enhance cost control over their projects. They need to have adequate experience, exposure, and training in financial analysis and measurement to support their responsibility to report project performance accurately.

COMMUNICATION SKILLS

Communication skills are universally recognized as essential for successful project managers. Because communication is the foundation for virtually all project management activities, some have even suggested that if a person lacks innate communication skills, he or she should be dissuaded from pursuing the project management career path. Several key aspects of communication skills are critical to project management success:

- *Information sharing.* In the absence of information, people will fill the void with assumptions, guesses, and their own biases. The project manager's ability to communicate effectively (both providing and receiving information) with key stakeholders and constituencies is a critical success factor on most projects. Key to successful communication is the ability to ask the right questions.

- *Engaging executives.* A primary role of the project manager is to protect the project—its funding, resources, scope, and schedule. Communicating effectively with executives is critical to ensuring project progress. To that end, project managers must engage executives to obtain agreement, support, guidance, and decisions. Those who successfully communicate with executives establish clear expectations at the outset of a project. They ask executives their preferred method, timing, and content of communication throughout the project and also outline the project's needs and expectations in terms of communication with the executive.

- *Negotiation.* Negotiation is the process whereby two or more parties with different needs and desired outcomes work to find a mutually acceptable solution. Since negotiating is an interpersonal process, each negotiating situation is different, influenced by each party's skills, attitudes, and style. People often regard negotiating as unpleasant because it suggests conflict. Understanding more about the process enables project managers to conduct negotiations with confidence and increases the likelihood that the outcomes will be positive for both parties.

  For organizations where most project staff is contracted, negotiation is a very practical project management skill, allowing the government to obtain the needed resources for the best price. On a more operational level, project managers spend most of their day negotiating—with other project managers to obtain resources, with executives to obtain approvals, with team members on tasks and schedules, and with vendors on pricing.

  Communicating Clearly. The most carefully thought-out communication plan and the best communication methods and tools will be worthless if the message is not clear. The project manager's goals are to understand and to be understood. To achieve these dual goals, the project manager must have the ability to communicate (in person and in writing) from the perspective of the project's constituents and stakeholder groups (e.g., IT, construction, budgets, contracts). This skill can be particularly challenging for project managers who come from technical areas, where writing clearly and succinctly may not have been as valued a skill.

- *Teaching and mentoring.* The ability to teach or mentor is an important skill that project managers must possess to support their projects. Regardless of their project management maturity level, most organizations rely on experienced project managers to teach and mentor rising project managers, team members, and even executives on project management practices and value. In some cases, the project manager provides "just-in-time" training on project management tasks and technical project elements.

SUBJECT MATTER EXPERTISE

The importance of a project manager's expertise in the project's "subject" depends on many factors, including the organization, the individual, the project team, and the project's level of complexity (see Figure 8-1).

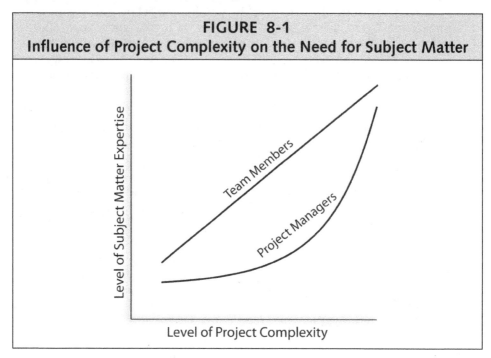

FIGURE 8-1
Influence of Project Complexity on the Need for Subject Matter

FAC-P/PM PROGRAM

In 2007 OMB launched the federal acquisition certification for program and project managers (FAC-P/PM). The certification is required for program and project managers that are assigned to major acquisitions. The model comprises seven competencies: [5]

1. Requirements development and management process
2. System engineering
3. Test and evaluation
4. Lifecycle logistics
5. Acquisition/contracting
6. Business financial management
7. Leadership/professional.

Performance outcomes are defined for each FAC-P/PM competency at all three levels of certification. These include task descriptions of what a program or project manager must be able to perform in order to demonstrate competence and excel in the program and project manager career field. For example, a senior-level performance outcome for the first competency (requirements development and management process) is to "synthesize the efforts and output of functionally oriented product/process teams in preparation for and execution of milestone and stakeholder reviews of the program."[6]

Although the FAC-P/PM certification is clearly acquisition-oriented, it is generally related to industry standards for project management skills, particularly those promoted by PMI (see Table 8-2). In fact, FAI has a "letter of understanding" with PMI to accept the CAPM® and PMP® credentials as satisfying the coursework areas and experience for the entry/apprentice and mid/journeyman levels of the FAC-P/PM.

TABLE 8-2 FAC-P/PM Levels and Skills[7]		
Project Manager Entry/Apprentice	**Program/Project Manager Mid/Journeyman**	**Program Manager Senior/Expert**
• Knowledge and skills to perform as a team member and manage low-risk and relatively simple projects with supervision	• Knowledge and skills to manage program/project segments of low to moderate risk with little or no supervision	• Knowledge and skills to manage and evaluate moderate to high-risk programs or projects and create an environment for program success
• Overall understanding of project management practices, including acquisition	• Ability to apply project management processes, including requirements and acquisition	• Ability to manage and evaluate the requirements development process, overseeing junior team members
• Ability to develop project management documents with supervision	• Ability to identify and track action to initiate an acquisition program/ project using cost/ benefit analysis	• Ability to use, manage, and evaluate management processes and techniques
• Knowledge of and involvement in the project requirements process	• Ability to support baseline reviews and total ownership cost estimates	• Ability to manage and evaluate the use of earned value management as it relates to acquisition investments

Certification under FAC-P/PM is purposely not centralized, in recognition of the "local" characteristics at the department and agency levels. Each agency is responsible for implementing a program that complies with the FAC-P/PM requirements, providing the necessary training, work experience, and skill development for its project managers.

Organizations that are ready to implement FAC-P/PM tend to have the following characteristics:

- Understand their workforce, their capabilities, and relevant skills
- Can identify personnel who are eligible to be certified
- Have a reasonably mature acquisition function
- Communicate and collaborate with their organization's acquisition personnel
- Can effectively manage the certified workforce after implementation.

For agencies that do not have formal project management structures, standards, or training, and where acquisitions are not the normal course of business, meeting OMB's goals for FAC-P/PM will be a greater challenge.

COMPETENCY DEVELOPMENT

Improving project management requires a commitment by the organization and its leaders to provide both formal and informal opportunities to increase the skills and knowledge of project managers. Some agencies have comprehensive training programs that integrate practical experience with skills and knowledge, leading toward internal project management certification. These programs include core courses, electives, and continuing education. Other approaches include contracting with external vendors to provide training or combining informal internal training with outside educational activities.

Manager Alert

Improving project management requires a commitment by the organization and its leaders to provide both formal and informal opportunities to increase the skills and knowledge of project managers.

For organizations that do not have a formal training or certification program, an informal approach to delivering training may be the best course to gain the executive support needed to implement a more formal program. Ideas for building momentum in the development of an organization's project management capabilities include four key areas:

- Training
- Coaching and mentoring
- On-the-job or just-in-time training
- Knowledge sharing.

The need for highly trained and certified project managers is increasing. As a project manager in your organization, you should endeavor to expand your knowledge and complement your experience with new, relevant skills, including seeking certification via your organization, PMI, or a master's degree program. Seek out and participate in relevant communities of practice, both face-to-face and online. Promote formal and information skill development in your organization; where the structures or activities do not exist, take the lead in establishing methods for improving project management skills.

The emergence of new skills that integrate with traditional skills will place increasing demands on federal project managers to adjust and adapt to new project environments. Acquiring and honing these skills will differentiate successful project managers and projects throughout the federal government.

NOTES

1. Statement of James A. Rispoli, Assistant Secretary for Environmental Management, U.S. Department of Energy, before the Subcommittee on Strategic Forces, Committee on Armed Services, U.S. House of Representatives, March 1, 2006.

2. Many GAO assessments and reports include references to management or project management practices. See GAO-08-1051T for several relevant citations in the information technology arena. Also, see the survey on project management skills, "The Council for Excellence in Government Program Management Survey Data Report" (Vienna, VA: Management Concepts, 2008).

3. "The Council for Excellence in Government Program Management Survey Data Report" (Vienna, VA: Management Concepts, 2008).

4. A Guide to the Project Management Body of Knowledge (PMBOK® Guide), Fifth Edition (Newtown Square, PA: Project Management Institute, 2013).

5. Federal Acquisition Institute, Certification FAC-P/PM, www.fai.gov/drupal/certification/program-and-project-managers-fac-ppm (accessed April 2013).

6. FAC-P/PM Competency Model Draft Version 1.9, June 13, 2012, www.fai.gov/drupal/sites/default/files/FAC-PPM%20Competency%20Model-Draftv1_9_13-June-2012_PDF.pdf (accessed April 2013).

7. Adapted from FAC-P/PM Draft Blueprint Version 1.2, October 15, 2007.

Chapter 9

THE FEDERAL PROJECT MANAGEMENT FRAMEWORK

You've got to think about the big things, so that all the small things go in the right directions.

—ALVIN TOFFLER, FUTURIST, AUTHOR

Many federal agencies have developed a project management framework that comprises three layers:

- *Organizational governance*—provides an open, structured format for evaluating investments and executive decision-making.
- *Project portfolio management*—provides a process for managing the inventory of work associated with specific parts of the organization.
- *Project management methodology*—involves the use of approaches and standards to manage the project environment.

Collectively, these three layers form a framework for effective project management. While most federal agencies make use of all three, the degree of coordination between the layers varies by agency.

ORGANIZATIONAL GOVERNANCE

Governance is a process that brings together agency leadership and managers to enable coordinated, open decision-making. The goal of governance is generally to provide a forum for internal stakeholders to participate in shaping the decisions and investments that will improve the performance of the organization. Governance is premised on the idea of scarcity—that there will never be enough resources to accomplish all the initiatives an agency would like to undertake. Given the dichotomy of limited resources and a plethora of good ideas, governance is a process that continually evaluates the investment portfolio to ensure that an agency is making the best choices based on a variety of criteria.

The function of governance sits above project management, spanning the full lifecycle of investment decision-making, from idea conception to evaluation, acquisition, project management, maintenance and operations, and retirement. Yet governance has a direct impact on the scope, scale, and budgets of projects. Projects are created, approved, renewed, or discontinued based on governance processes.

In the federal environment, governance takes a variety of forms. For example, governance can simply equate to a group of executives who meet regularly in the context of coordinated decision-making or it can comprise multiple layers of committees and formal processes within an agency. Depending on the scope of governance, it may be called "enterprise governance," "IT governance," or "investment review boards" (IRBs). As displayed in Figure 9-1, the typical governance structure is hierarchical, with an executive committee and multiple subcommittees. In this case, the executive committee would act as the IRB. Often, technical committees operate below the lines of business to reconcile the ideas and decisions of governance with specific implementation challenges.

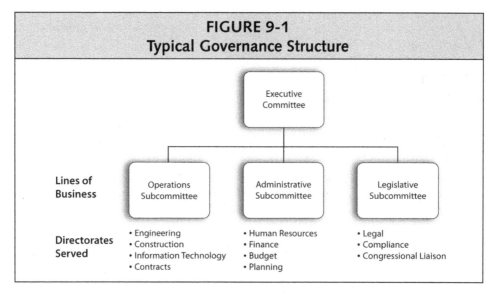

FIGURE 9-1
Typical Governance Structure

Governance also operates across multiple levels of the U.S. government. For example, there are governance structures specific to directorates within an agency, governance structures that span an entire agency, and even superstructures that span the entire government (such as the CIO Council). Information technology organizations are the most prevalent arena for governance, in part because IT investments require heavy input from across the organization to ensure effective implementation.

Governance is a balancing act that involves addressing the pressing priorities of the day while pursuing longer-term investments that will advance the agency as a whole. Often, governance makes investments from three "buckets"—*operate* the business, *improve* the business, and *transform* the business:

- *Operate.* This area is also known as "keeping the lights on." Operating the business involves maintaining the basic infrastructure of people, processes, physical plant, technology, and other areas that provide the agency with the basic tools to operate. These current, known obligations represent the largest area of expenditure for most agencies.

- *Improve.* To address current challenges, the agency must continuously improve and upgrade its physical plant, processes, technology, and people. These improvements do not represent wholesale change but are required for the efficient operation of the business. Improvements generally help keep the agency from falling behind in meeting customers' needs, and they can include upgrading technology, revising policy and procedure manuals, and modifying staffing.

- *Transform.* When an agency seeks to redesign an area of its business, it effectively transforms the business by redefining the basic assumptions, processes, and tools it uses to conduct business. Transformation may involve implementing new technologies, processes, or ways of dealing with customers. Transforming the business goes beyond improvements to existing systems, driving toward a complete rethinking of the agency's core processes.

Federal leaders must balance their investments across these three buckets, addressing the changing priorities of the organization. Within each bucket, federal governance processes should consider investments in terms of a variety of criteria:

- *Risk.* Agency leadership needs to understand the exposure incurred by a given investment, as well as across a band of investments. For example, investments in technology should align with the agency's overall risk profile.

- *Performance.* Projects and processes must meet performance standards, as defined by OMB, the agency, or the manufacturer (if a product is involved).

- *Transparency.* Transparency operates at two levels in governance. First, the federal agency must adhere to the letter and spirit of open government. The Presidential Memorandum dated January 21, 2009, requires executive agencies to "harness new technologies to put information about their operations and decisions online and readily available to the public."[1]

Second, governance provides an open forum for addressing the needs of all organizational stakeholders. This transparency is essential to ensuring that all voices are heard.

- *Legal and regulatory requirements.* According to OMB Circular A-11, Part 7:

  Agencies must develop, implement, and use a capital programming process to develop their capital asset portfolio, and must:

  o Evaluate and select capital asset investments that will support core mission functions...

  o Initiate improvements to existing assets or acquisitions of new assets only when no alternative private sector or governmental source can more efficiently meet the need

  o Simplify or otherwise redesign work processes to reduce costs, improve effectiveness...

  o Reduce project risk by avoiding or isolating custom designed components...

  o Structure major acquisitions into useful segments with a narrow scope and brief duration, make adequate use of competition and appropriately allocate risk between Government and contractor

  o Institute performance measures and management processes for monitoring and comparing actual performance to planned results.[2]

- *Ethics.* Governance plays an important role in allowing executives to have open debate on the ethics of one idea versus another (for example, the decision to fund one grant over another where each grant may result in real improvements to the human condition).

The governance process is most often used in the IT environment, where IRBs act as the primary mechanism for executing governance functions.

One complaint about governance structures is that the internal bureaucracy slows down decision-making. This is a legitimate concern, and governance committees need to be responsive to their stakeholders. One way to do this is to more closely engage key stakeholders and business owners in the process. Another is to develop expedited procedures for specific types of requests, such as those under a certain dollar threshold.

PROJECT PORTFOLIO MANAGEMENT

Portfolio management is the integrated coordination and oversight of selected groupings of projects (or investments). Portfolio management is integral to the work that is done in governance, with each providing inputs and outputs to the other. For example, portfolio management produces the critical performance and financial/resource data that executives need to perform the governance function. In governance, executives make decisions that impact the portfolio. These decisions must be integrated back into each project in the portfolio, and the overall portfolio must then be re-calibrated.

In the federal government, governance and portfolio management tend to be tightly coupled within agencies. Agencies that have invested in one of these functions typically have a robust process for the other as well.

Particular features differentiate portfolios from a simple grouping of projects. For example, portfolios have the following:

- *A portfolio manager.* An accountable person is charged with the overall health and well-being of the portfolio.

- *Defined boundaries.* Portfolios are defined by their budgets, scope of investments, and organizational boundaries.

- *Criteria for inclusion.* To be accepted into the portfolio, a project or investment must meet certain criteria, such as a risk score.

- *Integrated reporting.* Portfolios tend to be tallied and examined en masse so that executives and others can view the totality of the portfolio across different dimensions (e.g., resources, budget, demand, performance).

Portfolios often address the full lifecycle of the asset—selection and planning, implementation and control, operations and maintenance, and eventually retirement. Project management informs part of the lifespan of the asset but usually stops at operations and maintenance and retirement. In other words, at some point the asset is no longer a project but a depreciating asset "owned" by a business unit that is part of the unit's annual budget.

Portfolio managers perform much of the nuts-and-bolts work required to enable governance-level decision-making: calculating EVM, producing reports, and interfacing with other systems like HR and accounting. The portfolio manager must endeavor to integrate key management interfaces, such as:

- *Strategic plan:* ensure that the portfolio addresses division, agency, and governmental priorities.

- *Risk:* manage the individual and cumulative exposure of the investment portfolio.

- *Architecture:* verify that projects adhere to the overall architectural guidance, as defined in the federal enterprise architecture (FEA). Each agency maintains a plan that adheres to the FEA.

- *Portfolio management strategy:* ensure that investment prioritization techniques are robust and valid for the organization.

- *Inventory:* incorporate clear boundaries and reconcile with the budgets associated with the portfolio.

A single portfolio comprises multiple projects and programs. Yet the portfolio itself should have an objective. After all, why group these particular items together? Generally, portfolios are created around functional units, such as IT, or around budgetary items, such as funding for a specific purpose. For example, an IT portfolio may have as its objective the efficient use of IT investment dollars. Project portfolios must address the notion of tradeoffs over time, such as how much to invest now versus later. Moreover, portfolios need to incorporate specific processes around performance management, risk management, and investment management.[3]

Figure 9-2 depicts an approach to project portfolio management that supports the governance process. In proposal support, investment ideas are gathered and processed for selection. This function is sometimes referred to as "demand management," and indeed, that is what is happening. In any organization, there is no shortage of good ideas, so the proposal support process allows for these good ideas to be developed iteratively without necessarily requiring a significant commitment from the organization. Following proposal support comes governance support, whereby the portfolio is made ready for governance review via report production, data verification, agenda development, etc. Also, governance committees are often managed as a function of governance support. This means that the committees are scheduled, facilitated, and documented by the portfolio management team. Finally, inventory management occurs, whereby the portfolio is assessed and adjusted to reconcile governance decisions as well as changes in project and program baselines.

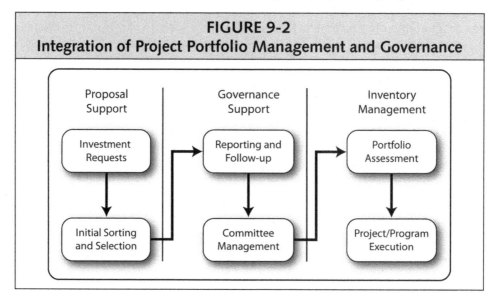

FIGURE 9-2
Integration of Project Portfolio Management and Governance

Portfolio management should create efficiencies across projects through macro-level resource management. Inventory management seeks to understand key aspects of the portfolio, including:

- The skills and abilities needed across the portfolio
- Whether the current portfolio of projects addresses the agency's major growth areas adequately
- The major risks across the portfolio
- How individual projects in the portfolio are performing.

Manager Alert

Effective portfolio management can create efficiencies across projects through macro-level resource management.

Portfolio management often exacerbates the challenges associated with managing large organizations. In the federal environment, agency leadership teams continue to struggle with integrated strategic decision-making on several fronts:

- *Too much information.* Executives faced with strategic decision-making authority must process enormous amounts of information. This can include laws, regulations, performance reports, analyses, projections and estimates, and past decisions. The sheer amount of information makes it hard to differentiate the truly important data from the less important.

- *Not enough input from business stakeholders.* Sometimes, as a result of too much information, stakeholders get locked out of the process. In a sense, the portfolio really belongs to those business stakeholders, yet their input is sometimes sought out too late or too quickly, with poor results.

- *Inadequate processes.* The portfolio management and governance processes need to be bolstered with adequate processes and tools to be able to handle the budget issues, power struggles, and other calamities that befall the portfolio in any given year.

- *Conflicting internal priorities.* Investment management requires tenacity and conviction to see an investment through in the face of tough budget shortfalls and important near-term goals. Yet again, executives must also understand when to cut an investment and redefine priorities.

Despite these challenges, a new generation of project portfolio management tools is emerging. These tools facilitate EVM, resource management, streamlined information (through dashboards), and related portfolio functions. Many federal agencies are recognizing that portfolio management is a data-intensive effort and that robust tools are a key differentiator between mediocrity and a successful portfolio management approach.

PROJECT MANAGEMENT METHODOLOGY

At the individual project level, a methodology provides guidance and coordination to the team. A project management methodology defines the structure for moving through the stages of a project. A methodology can provide a set of templates that will aid in the development of a consistent approach to doing the work, a common language, and predictable outputs.

Most federal agencies have adopted or developed a project management methodology in some part of their organization. Yet many organizations within agencies still struggle with the basic tenets of implementing project management.

Project management methodologies are products of their environment. No two are exactly the same, in part because of differences in culture and organizational structure. Agencies must strive to tailor their project management methodology to their business practices in a meaningful way.

Two methodologies commonly used in the federal environment are the waterfall methodology and the agile methodology.

Waterfall Methodology

Many projects in the federal environment follow a waterfall approach, whereby discovery leads to design, which then informs implementation, validation, and closeout. These phases each tend to be completed once in a project, with little iteration. This is the classic project management methodology—the "the archetypal project cycle model from which all others derived . . . ."[4]

As Figure 9-3 shows, the waterfall methodology relies upon earlier work to be completed for later work to proceed. One strength of this approach is that emphasis is placed on getting the up-front discovery done correctly. Conversely, a weakness is that if a team does a poor job gathering requirements, the resulting system will reflect incomplete or poor-quality requirements.

Because the waterfall approach is sequential, it involves substantial documentation. This reliance on capturing information at a point in time can lead to problems as requirements change. Project management leadership needs to construct processes that allow for review and update of the requirements in later phases of the project, suggesting a modified waterfall approach. In a modified waterfall approach, iterative loops allow for feedback on specific content areas, like requirements, that are typically generated very early in the project.

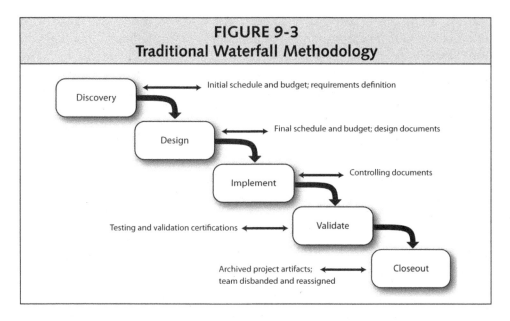

FIGURE 9-3
Traditional Waterfall Methodology

Discovery → Initial schedule and budget; requirements definition

Design → Final schedule and budget; design documents

Implement → Controlling documents

Testing and validation certifications ← Validate

Archived project artifacts; ← Closeout
team disbanded and reassigned

Agile Methodology

The agile methodology was originally conceived for application development. Yet project management has adopted its tenets and agile as PM is gaining some ground as an alternative to the traditional waterfall approach to projects. Agile project management is a way to "energize, empower, and enable project teams to rapidly and reliably deliver business value by engaging customers and continuously learning and adapting to their changing needs and environments."[5] The founders of this approach promote the following four tenets in their "Manifesto for Agile Software Development":

1. Individuals and interactions over processes and tools

2. Working software over comprehensive documentation

3. Customer collaboration over contract negotiation

4. Responding to change over following a plan.[6]

These founding principles may seem counter to the operation of government enterprises, with their regulated structure and high levels of accountability. However, the flexible nature of agile project management requires the discipline and structure that some more mature project organizations can provide.

Agile project managers have to achieve a balance between emergent order and imposed order. While imposed order is a top-down approach to organizational control, emergent order uses a bottom-up approach. Successful project managers will use a mixture of imposed and emergent order to achieve an ideal work environment. To accomplish this balance, project managers should undertake the following actions:

- Collaborate with stakeholders to understand the vision for the project, how it aligns with the goals of the organization, and how it will be used. Information flow is needed at all stages of agile management because any problems will have to be corrected quickly.

- Organize a group discussion with the team to generate a common project vision. This is the first step toward establishing the teamwork needed.

- Identify, communicate, and maintain this guiding vision.

- Establish a planning process that defines the purpose and goals while giving team members autonomy and allowing team innovation.

- Implement a flexible management approach based on observation as well as planning. A project manager who has visionary leadership is continuously observing, learning, and acclimating to the environment.

Manager Alert

Agile project managers have to achieve a balance between emergent order and imposed order.

While agile project management adds speed and flexibility to sound project management practices, the "radical" nature of this approach may be too large a leap for some organizations steeped in more traditional project management methodologies. However, applying some of the agile principles can fill the gap between the "chaos" of the agile approach and the highly structured waterfall method.

Many federal agencies have adopted the basic practices of governance and project portfolio management within their IT environments. Looking ahead, agencies need to develop more effective methods of integrating these disciplines with project management methodologies. A more coordinated approach to managing investments is critical, especially in these tough economic times. Project management leadership must take the lead in bridging the divide between internal teams and their customers, executives and staff, and agency goals and individual actions.

Successful agencies are proactively pursuing new ways of doing business. To support these innovations, agencies need robust governance and portfolio tools. For example, new portfolio management tools are providing insights into resource constraints and high-risk projects. Agencies that devote resources to improving governance and portfolio management will realize the results of streamlined decision processes and higher-quality investments. The savings realized will enable more efficient operations. The future is bright for agencies that maximize the efficient use of the core processes of governance and portfolio management.

NOTES

1.   Memorandum for the Heads of Executive Departments and Agencies, January 21, 2009, www.whitehouse.gov/the_press_office/Transparency_and_Open_Government (accessed April 2013).

2.   OMB Circular No. A–11 Part 7, Planning, Budgeting, Acquisition, and Management of Capital Assets, p. 7.

3.   www.army.mil/ArmyBTKC/gov/pfm.htm (accessed April 2013).

4.   Kathleen B. Hass, *Managing Complex Projects* (Vienna, VA: Management Concepts, 2009), p.84.

5.   Sanjiv Augustine, *Managing Agile Projects* (Upper Saddle River, NJ: Prentice Hall, 2005), p. 23.

6.   "Manifesto for Agile Software Development," www.agilemanifesto.org (accessed April 2013).

Chapter 10

UNDERSTANDING PROJECT PERFORMANCE MANAGEMENT

> *In the social sectors, the critical question is not "how much money do we make per dollar of invested capital?" but "how effectively do we deliver on our mission and make a distinctive impact, relative to our resources?"*
>
> —JIM COLLINS, *GOOD TO GREAT AND THE SOCIAL SECTORS*

Tracking investment dollars is a familiar activity in the federal environment. Yet it remains unclear how much value the federal government and American taxpayers receive from the massive investment in projects. The performance management framework that operates in the federal environment can shed some light on this value.

PERFORMANCE MANAGEMENT IN THE FEDERAL GOVERNMENT

The federal government uses a variety of tools to manage performance, including E-300s, GAO's high-risk list, IT scorecards, variance reports, and corrective action plans. Cost, schedule, and performance goals must be established for all major acquisitions, and agencies must achieve, on average, 90 percent of those goals. OMB Circular A-11, Part 7, provides a critical source of guidance in its Capital Programming Guide supplement, which lays out the important acquisition steps and identifies earned value as a method of measuring project progress. In total, these systemic changes to performance management have brought about improvements to the methods agencies use to establish strategic goals, work with contractors, use performance data, and manage projects.

Performance-based management involves establishing, managing, measuring, and evaluating performance data. Project performance must link into the overall performance management program, and the organization must ensure that projects can be measured individually and in tandem with other projects in the portfolio. This is a significant challenge for many agencies.

Success in project management in the federal environment involves recognizing the following:

- Performance management is multidimensional, requiring collaboration and coordination between acquisition, finance, operations, policy and planning, human resources, oversight, and other agency divisions.

- Performance management involves all levels of the government, from the single project to agency executives, OMB, and Congress.

- Performance management is predicated on the effective implementation of earned value management.

- At the heart of effective performance management is good data, including information about the reliability of the data.

- EVM and project management systems have evolved to the point where effective project reporting can be accomplished by agencies with limited project management expertise.

The primary focus of the performance-based management strategy has been on major IT systems and the use of earned value management to monitor progress. While EVM and its predecessors have been in use in the federal government since the 1960s, EVM is only now gaining widespread traction across both defense and civilian agencies. The government continues to develop the performance management capability to ensure that capital investments are performing well.

IMPROVING PROJECT PERFORMANCE

In the context of the broader federal performance measurement system, project performance management offers opportunities for agencies to improve project performance management across three phases of a project:

- *Establish project performance measures.* Performance systems are developed at the organizational level, and baselines are put into place at the project level.

- *Manage project performance.* Effective performance management strategies help establish a rigor within the project team.

- *Oversee project performance.* An independent oversight board examines the project to verify that performance is on target and that the underlying systems and data are adequate.

Each of these phases lends itself to an overall system of project performance management. Each fits into the larger flow of performance data that flows upward from project to agency to government-wide performance scorecards, and ultimately to congressional hearings.

Establishing Project Performance Measures

As the old adage goes, "If you can't measure it, you can't move it." Performance measurement systems should enable a project manager to closely monitor the project and enact changes. Establishing performance measures in a project environment involves creating measures at the individual, work team, and project levels, as well as creating policies and the operational framework to ensure that high-quality performance data is generated. To ensure a successful project performance measurement program, the sponsor and key agency leadership need to consider three key areas that will enable a full-fledged performance management system: investment review boards, EVM, and non-EVM performance criteria.

Manager Alert

Establishing performance measures in a project environment involves creating measures at the individual, work team, and project levels.

Investment Review Boards

At the organizational level, the agency must create an environment conducive to high performance. For example, in IT projects, OMB has recommended the use of an IT investment management (ITIM) maturity framework, whereby the agency creates one or more investment review boards, or IRBs, to oversee the development of IT investments.

The IRB is a common mechanism in agencies for bringing together IT and business executives in a process to define and understand the investment. The investment has to be clearly understood in terms of both its costs and its benefits by all stakeholders. Under this framework, IRBs consider new projects and reevaluate prior investments to ensure they are on track. To do this, IRBs must establish new performance baselines and evaluate existing project performance data.

The ITIM framework is not without challenges. IRBs must have the right people involved in the process. To be effective, senior directors from across the organization must participate in the process. Because the IRB is a decision-making body, delegating IRB meetings to lower-level staff is not a good practice. These boards must also have the right technical and nontechnical staff in attendance. The complexity of these investments, and their success, sometimes rests upon arcane technical details that will make or break the investment.

The IRB must also have the right processes in place for considering new investments, reviewing existing investments, and assessing performance. When those processes are not in place, investments can be ignored or left unanalyzed. In addition, when corrective actions are called for, the IRB must be prepared to track the completion of those actions. GAO recommends that agencies "strengthen and expand the board's oversight responsibilities for underperforming projects . . . ."[1] These challenges are longstanding, but clearly the ITIM framework, and the IRBs, allow for continuous evaluation of project performance data at the appropriate levels of the agency.

Earned Value Management

At the heart of performance management in the federal government is earned value, based on ANSI/EIA standard 748 (2007). Earned value is a project management concept whereby the value of the work completed in a given period is compared with the planned value of the work and the actual value of the work. Cost and schedule data are used to help understand the true performance of a project. For example, if a project team completed a new $2 million parking lot at an actual cost of $3 million, there would be a –$1 million cost variance.

Schedule data also informs the performance data and uses the earned value of work for a given time period as compared with what was expected to be completed at the end of the time period. For example, if, at the end of the month, the project team has completed $1 million of the work, but was budgeted to have completed $1.1 million, the project would have a –$100,000 schedule variance.

The objective is to understand the planned value of the work at any given point—the earned value. This level of information provides executives and stakeholders across the government a look into the status and overall health of the project.

The DOD 2006 *Earned Value Management Implementation Guide* provides details on what EVM can accomplish.[2] The guide states that an EVM system (EVMS) allows for the following:

- Planning of all work scope for the program to completion
- Assignment of authority and responsibility at the work performance level
- Integration of the cost, schedule, and technical aspects of the work into a detailed baseline plan
- Objective measurement of progress (earned value) at the work performance level

- Accumulation and assignment of actual costs
- Analysis of variances from plans
- Summarization and reporting of performance data to higher levels of management for action
- Forecasting of achievement of milestones and completion of contract events
- Forecasting of final contract costs
- Disciplined baseline maintenance and incorporation of baseline revisions in a timely manner.

On the civilian side of the federal government, only a handful of agencies have vigorously embraced EVM for many years, including NASA and DOE. These agencies adopted the American National Standards Institute/Electronics Industries Alliance national standard for EVM, called ANSI/EIA-748, which provides the "industry process for the use of EVMS including integration of program scope, schedule and cost objectives, establishment of a baseline plan and accomplishment of program objectives, and use of earned value techniques for performance measurement during the execution of a program."[3]

Federal management and acquisition teams have begun to focus on EVM in recent years. EVM can be used as a stand-alone system or in conjunction with other measurement methods. It can be applied at various levels, from individual projects all the way up to cabinet-level department initiatives.

Earned value relies on extensive data—including direct labor data, materials cost data, schedule data, indirect cost data, and contract data—from a wide variety of sources. The systems that enable earned value are complex, and in the case of contractors, must be certified by the federal government as appropriate for use as an EVM tool. An EVMS must be aligned with the organization and its resources to ensure the proper allocation of work. The organizational breakdown structure (OBS) is essential to linking work with specific organizational units. The resource breakdown structure (RBS) accomplishes a similar objective, but with project resources.

The first step in defining an effective EVMS is to overlay the WBS, OBS, and RBS. In other words, effort should be catalogued by its WBS reference number, assigned organization, and actual resources used. The project manager will thereby be able to track performance across those various elements.

> Any federal EVM implementation must adhere to ANSI/EIA-748. The standard sets forth 32 guidelines that enable EVM systems implementation. To be compliant, an EVM system must address all 32 guidelines, which cover such items as (1) "Define the authorized work elements for the program," (16) "Record direct costs in a manner consistent with the budgets in a formal system controlled by the general books of account," and (31) "Prevent revisions to the program budget, except for authorized changes."[4]

A fully compliant system is no small feat, as the guidelines address organizational structure; accounting, budgeting, and finance; project management; and human resources. Additionally, OMB has established "key practices" supporting systems acquisition programs, summarized into three areas:

1.   Establish a comprehensive EVM system.

2.   Ensure that the data resulting from the EVM system are reliable.

3.   Ensure that the program management team is using earned value data for decision-making purposes.

While the three areas are interdependent and each area is important, the third is the most critical for the agency. EVM helps ensure that better decisions are made through the integration of performance data.

Non-EVM Performance Criteria

EVM provides essential performance data; however, the project also maintains other performance criteria that are important to evaluating the overall success of the effort. For example, safety performance criteria are not necessarily embedded within the EVM calculation, although injuries and work slowdowns due to unsafe conditions will impact project performance. The team may have a performance criterion that states "This project will incur zero accidents until its completion." This is a goal that is separate and apart from the performance of the project, but it should nonetheless be used to evaluate the overall success of the effort.

Another example is training. Ensuring that all project staff receive proper training can be tracked as a separate performance measure even though it will impact overall project performance. Training will probably be built into the schedule, so if it is not completed on time, it will directly impact the EVM calculation. Viewed separately, untrained staff members lead to poor-quality deliverables and rework, so clearly training impacts performance. Moreover, the organization will not be prepared to maintain and operate the final deliverables if staff members have not received the proper training. So tracking training goals as a separate performance measure provides a meaningful way to realize the outcomes of the project.

If a project manager maintains a zero variance for cost and schedule, but does so because the project is hiring lower-quality labor and not providing safety equipment or training, the project's risk profile will increase. Non-EVM performance criteria should drive decisions about tasks, budgets, and time frames. These are important filters for understanding how projects are faring.

Managing Project Performance

Performance management goes hand in hand with project management. The project team executes on the plan and generates the performance results. Invariably, problems that degrade the performance of the project arise. For example, resource shortages may occur or the cost of materials may increase. Sometimes these issues were planned for and alternatives can be implemented with minimal disruption. Other times these circumstances occur without foreknowledge and the team must scramble to get back on track. In either case, an effective management strategy must be followed to ensure that project performance is monitored and corrected as necessary.

Manager Alert
Performance management goes hand in hand with project management.

Performance management is cyclical, with each turn presenting opportunities for improvement.

These opportunities include the following:

- *Maintain accountability.* An effective project performance strategy begins with accountability. The project manager must know his or her role and responsibilities, as should the rest of the team. Individuals should be accountable for specific outcomes and results. Accountability is the precursor of ownership, which is a critical element in performance. In short, today's knowledge workers must care or performance will likely degrade.

- *Actively monitor.* A performance management strategy also requires an effective monitoring plan. Performance should be monitored and evaluated regularly through performance reports, post-implementation reviews, and on-site reviews. Yet, performance issues do not always come from reports, but often arise from direct observations and interactions with staff. The project team needs to be able to discuss performance issues honestly without defensiveness or fear of retribution.

- *Regularly measure.* Performance measurement is the mechanism for collecting, reporting, analyzing, and evaluating project performance data. The data used in many federal systems has been noted as suspect, due to poor collection processes.

- *Take corrective action.* Next, the team needs the ability to respond to performance issues. The team should be empowered to act on the performance data within the parameters of its responsibilities. For some federal projects, this may mean implementing contingency plans. In other instances, it may require executing scenario-based training. Corrective action should address the core issues related to performance.

While many different strategies will be effective in managing performance, this straightforward set of steps can enable federal managers to positively impact their projects.

Overseeing Project Performance

The federal government has invested in tracking tools designed to oversee projects and programs that aren't meeting performance goals. Early detection and correction of problems, while the project is underway, is becoming a best practice in federal projects. In recent years, increased emphasis has been placed on measuring projects more consistently. OMB retains much of the responsibility for implementing programs that will result in improvements. For example, OMB now requires that all large projects use an earned value management system. On the congressional side of the measurement spectrum, GAO provides oversight and accountability in its reviews of individual programs and agency results.

OMB's role in project performance has been increasing in recent years, through the use of such tools as the Program Assessment Rating Tool, Exhibit 300, and performance dashboards. These tools are evolving into effective instruments for tracking and improving project performance. Further, OMB has the authority to impose consequences if agencies do not deliver.

Not only does OMB's scorecard include traditional data elements, but it posts photographs of the agency CIOs. The intent of putting a literal face to senior management is to drive accountability throughout the entire agency.

OMB leadership has clearly come to realize that project performance management is an ongoing process. Project evaluation and measurement, both during and after projects, are conducted not just to identify and correct errors but also to determine and evaluate what worked and how successful methods might be replicated.

Federal project managers and their contractor counterparts are faced with a dilemma of divergence. On the one hand, projects are rapidly increasing in complexity. From legislative and regulatory requirements to technical challenges, the level of project complexity has never been greater. On the other hand, stakeholders are demanding more and more for their tax dollars. Citizens and lawmakers alike understand that projects must deliver value, and they have the tools to be heard.

Project performance management starts at the agency level. To be successful in the federal environment, agency leadership would do well to understand how EVM works. Pursuing performance management takes courage and conviction because it will invariably show areas where performance can be improved. Yet, it must be done. As projects take up more time, dollars, and operational space, it is important to build the proper support structure to be able to manage new initiatives as effectively as possible.

NOTES

1. U.S. Government Accountability Office, "Federal Agencies Need to Strengthen Investment Board Oversight of Poorly Planned and Performing Projects," GAO Report 09-566, June 2007, p.7.

2. U.S. Department of Defense, *Earned Value Management Implementation Guide,* October 2006, p. 3.

3. Federal CIO Council, "A Framework for Developing Earned Value Management Systems (EVMS) Policy for Information Technology Projects," December 5, 2005.

4. Federal CIO Council.

Chapter 11

THE PROMISE OF PROJECT MANAGEMENT IN THE FEDERAL GOVERNMENT

There is no quick road to project management maturity, but with perseverance and a thick skin, much can be done.

—ALLAN ROIT, FORMER DIRECTOR, FINANCIAL CRIMES
ENFORCEMENT NETWORK, U.S. DEPARTMENT OF THE TREASURY

Among the things Americans expect, today more than ever, is effective government. Regardless of methods or tools, fundamental project management structures and individual skills are the key drivers to project success in the federal government. On a more macro level, the discipline of project management is a primary means of creating more effective government. What lies ahead for project management in the federal government?

The state of project management in the federal government varies from agency to agency. Yet, several trends are evident in the federal project management arena. These trends do not represent the sum total of the future of project management in the federal government, but they do indicate the direction project management is taking. Those on the front lines offer some insights and ideas for improving the discipline of project management across the federal government.

PERSPECTIVES ON KEY TRENDS AND LESSONS LEARNED

Successful practices are being implemented across a broad range of federal organizations. These success stories provide lessons learned for organizations looking to implement or improve their project management practices, tools, skills, and techniques.

Organization and Structure

Some of the greatest strides in federal project management are likely to be in the area of organization and structure. The increasing interest and oversight demonstrated by Congress through hearings and legislation, OMB through initiatives such as FAC-P/PM, and GAO through its high-risk list will likely promote the formalization of project management organizations and structures within federal agencies, though not likely standardization across departments.

Implementation of formal governance processes, establishment of enterprise-level PMOs, increased accountability, and greater centralization of project management across the federal government are current trends emerging in this arena. The massive infusion of funding and projects initiated through ARRA have accelerated these trends, as requirements for close management, tracking, and reporting on the results were attached to the money. The increased level of visibility into projects across the entire federal government is readily apparent at www.Recovery.gov.

The continued growth and maturation of PMOs has provided an opportunity and a target for the discipline in the federal government. While PMOs remain an appropriate and important enabler of project success, their existence is threatened when project performance continues to underwhelm executives and key stakeholders, especially those that control budgets. PMO leaders and those working to implement PMOs in their organizations must be sure they work closely with executives and stakeholders to set reasonable expectations and build in the appropriate training and portfolio and governance processes suitable for their organization and culture.

People

While many trends are affecting the "people" component of project management in the federal government, such as the aging workforce and the economy, two areas are receiving particular attention: stakeholders and skill and practice development.

Stakeholders

Project stakeholders are becoming increasingly sophisticated. Greater access to information has piqued their higher levels of interest and engagement. In response, project managers must develop comprehensive communication strategies that employ both traditional techniques and emerging technologies. Beyond increased communication, project managers will find themselves integrating key stakeholders more directly into activities throughout the project lifecycle.

Manager Alert

Failing to meet stakeholders' expectations for greater involvement can derail a project or distract the project manager from more critical project tasks.

Skill and Practice Development

The key trends related to project management skills and practices are the formalization of training and certification, expansion of the government-wide project management community to proliferate best practices, and specialization in project management. Increasingly, organizations will support certification of project management personnel initially resulting from mandates, such as the FAC-P/PM requirements, but ultimately because agency executives and project sponsors will understand that improved professional competency helps the individual, the organization, and the government at large.

Along with the focus on improving skills, organizations are likely to codify the role of the project manager by establishing a career path and including project management responsibilities as part of personnel performance reviews. This emphasis on project management specialization will lead to the emergence of PM roles in functional units across agencies and increased participation in project management communities of practice or relevant functional areas (e.g., construction, IT, social services). These communities are growing within government agencies and in industry at large.

Process

Improvements to project management practices are being implemented across the federal government. One area likely to experience continued and significant change is knowledge.

The broad category of knowledge addresses the quality, volume, access, and use of information. The more sophisticated stakeholders become, the greater their demand for better information that is easily and rapidly accessible. Similarly, the increasing complexity of projects—in terms of size, scope, and products—requires that project knowledge be shared across organizational and geographic boundaries. The effort to collect and disseminate lessons learned can no longer be relegated to the end of the project and only if time and resources permit.

A key driver in the improvement in project knowledge is technology. Technology is only a tool, but one that can vastly improve project management, particularly in support of communication and project evaluation. Intranet-based tools such as project management portals, which are becoming more commonplace, will support improved communication efforts. As the technology matures and proliferates, social networking tools will be applied in the management of projects to mirror the way communication is evolving in society. Project tracking and evaluation tools that support functions like EVM will also come into widespread use, driven in part by OMB requirements.

Again, the web will play an important part in spreading project knowledge. Sites like www.ExpectMore.gov provide unprecedented insight into government project successes and failures. Recovery.gov provides similar information regarding ARRA-funded projects.

THE MORE THINGS CHANGE . . .

Despite these clear trends in government project management, some things are not likely to change as a result of time, technology, or regulations:

- *People.* At the end of the day, projects involve people and people are unique. While the methods may evolve (e.g., web, messaging, tweeting), the techniques for managing, motivating, directing, and guiding project participants or stakeholders will likely not change much over time. Project managers must be able to deal with the good, the bad, and the ugly side of human nature, honing their own skills and capabilities.

- *Managing change.* The one thing guaranteed not to change is that change will always occur. Project management–related processes, structures, and technologies in particular will continue in a state of flux, challenging organizations and project managers to keep pace, adopt, and adapt. The ability to remain flexible and creative will continue to be an essential attribute of the successful project manager. Furthermore, project managers, team members, and key stakeholders will remain the primary catalysts or change agents responsible for preparing their colleagues and their organizations for the changes resulting from projects. Project managers will need to become adept at identifying and implementing formal change management processes and tools to increase their projects' likelihood of success.

- *Tools of the trade.* Gadgets and gizmos may have their appeal, but flip charts, sticky notes, pens, and notepads rarely crash and most people are adept at using them all. While meetings may become increasingly virtual, gathering a group around a table to get work done will always be an integral part of projects. Thus, the project manager's ability as facilitator and effective meeting leader will remain a key skill. The ability to define a task clearly and work a group through the process to achieve the desired outcome will remain essential.

- *Communicate, communicate, communicate.* Again, the methods may change over time, but the successful project manager must be a skillful communicator. The project manager and key team members must be able to deliver, receive, and process information from a variety of sources and formats.

Manager Alert

The ability to remain flexible and creative is an essential attribute of the successful project manager.

THE OUTLOOK FOR PROJECT MANAGEMENT IN THE FEDERAL GOVERNMENT

For some, raising project management to a prominent and critical position within their organizations is a success story; for others, it is a work in progress. Clearly, the practice and performance of project management are on the rise throughout the federal government.

The challenge remains to demonstrate the value of project management. While the meaning of "value" may be elusive, the success of projects is not when measured by timely and cost-effective delivery of expected results. Congressman Elijah Cummings, senior member of the House Committee on Oversight and Government Reform, sums it up best: "Mediocrity is expensive! The cost of executing projects poorly is significantly greater than investing in effective project performance."

Project management is increasingly being viewed as a critical skill set in the federal government. A new breed of manager is emerging—one that was raised on the precepts of project management and is comfortable in an environment characterized by frequent and rapid change. Federal project management is maturing, evolving from a purely homespun set of practices into a formal discipline within departments and across the government enterprise.

Manager Alert

Project management is increasingly viewed as a critical skill set in the federal government.

Considering the full scope of project management within the federal environment is overwhelming. But executives, sponsors, and project managers can take to heart one consistent lesson learned: success breeds success. Take manageable steps to build and improve project management in your organization, and you will find that you have contributed to achieving project management success in the federal government.

ACRONYMS AND ABBREVIATIONS

ARRA	American Recovery and Reinvestment Act of 2009
C/SCSC	cost and schedule control system criteria
CAO	chief administrative officer
CIO	chief information officer
COTR	contracting officer's technical representative
CPM	critical path methodology
DAU	Defense Acquisition University
DAWIA	Defense Acquisition Workforce Improvement Act
DoD	Department of Defense
DOE	Department of Energy
EVM	earned value management
EVMS	earned value management system
FAC-P/PM	federal acquisition certification for program and project management
FAI	Federal Acquisition Institute
FEA	federal enterprise architecture
FOIA	Freedom of Information Act
GAO	Government Accountability Office
IPT	integrated project team
IRB	investment review board
ITIM	IT investment management
LOB	line of business
MOST	management operation system technique
NGO	nongovernmental organization

OBS	organizational breakdown structure
OFPP	Office of Federal Procurement Policy
OMB	Office of Management and Budget
PERT	project evaluation and review technique
PgMO	program management office
PMI	Project Management Institute
PMBOK®	*A Guide to the Project Management Body of Knowledge*
PMO	project management office
RBS	resource breakdown structure
WBS	work breakdown structure

REFERENCES AND RESOURCES

Augustine, Sanjiv. *Managing Agile Projects.* Upper Saddle River, NJ: Prentice Hall, 2005.

Benton, D. A. *CEO Material: How to Be a Leader in Any Organization.* New York: McGraw Hill, 2009.

Budd, Charles I., and Charlene S. Budd. *A Practical Guide to Earned Value Project Management, Second Edition,* Vienna, VA: Management Concepts, 2010.

Cleland, David I., and Lewis R. Ireland. *Project Management Handbook: Applying Best Practices Across Global Industries.* New York: McGraw Hill, 2008.

Cleland, David I., and Lewis R. Ireland. *Project Management: Strategic Design and Implementation.* New York: McGraw-Hill, 2008.

Collins, Jim. *Good to Great: Why Some Companies Make the Leap . . . and Others Don't.* New York: HarperBusiness, 2001.

Duarte, Deborah L., and Nancy Tennant Snyder. *Virtual Team Critical Success.* Hoboken, NJ: John Wiley & Sons, 2003.

Federal Chief Information Officers Council. "A Framework for Developing Earned Value Management Systems (EVMS) Policy for Information Technology Projects," December 5, 2005.

Frame, J. Davidson. *Project Management Competences.* San Francisco: Jossey-Bass, 1999.

Hass, Kathleen B. *Managing Complex Projects: A New Model.* Vienna, VA: Management Concepts, 2009.

Haugan, Gregory T. *Project Planning and Scheduling.* Vienna, VA: Management Concepts, 2002.

Haugan, Gregory T. *The Work Breakdown Structure in Government Contracting.* Vienna, VA: Management Concepts, 2003.

Highsmith, Jim. *Agile Project Management: Creating Innovative Products.* Upper Saddle River: NJ: Pearson Education, 2004.

Irwin, Brian. *Managing Politics and Conflicts in Projects.* Vienna, VA: Management Concepts, 2008.

Jaques, Timothy, and Jonathan Weinstein. *Achieving Project Management Success in the Federal Government*. Vienna, VA: Management Concepts, 2010.

Morris, Rick A. *The Everything Project Management Book*. Avon, MA: Avon Media, 2008.

Newcomer, Kathryn E., and Barry White. *Getting Results: A Guide for Federal Leaders and Managers*. Vienna, VA: Management Concepts and Center for Innovation in Public Service, 2005.

Project Management Institute. *A Guide to the Project Management Body of Knowledge (PMBOK® Guide), Fifth Edition*. Newtown Square, PA: Project Management Institute, 2013.

Tuckman, Bruce W. "Developmental Sequence in Small Groups," *Psychological Bulletin*, 63, 384–399. Reprinted in *Group Facilitation: A Research and Applications Journal*, no. 3, Spring 2001.

U.S. Government Accountability Office. "21st Century Challenges: Reexamining the Base of the Federal Government," GAO-05-325SP. Washington, DC: U.S. Government Printing Office, February 2005.

U.S. Government Accountability Office. "Better Performance Information Needed to Support Agency Contract Award Decisions," GAO-09-374. Washington, DC: U.S. Government Printing Office, April 2009.

U.S. Government Accountability Office. "High Risk Series: An Update," GAO-13-283. Washington, DC: U.S. Government Printing Office, February 2013.

INDEX